...n ...g

A ha...rs

Peter Branston and Mark Provis

HODDER AND STOUGHTON
LONDON SYDNEY AUCKLAND TORONTO

To all children learning to read—
we hope this book makes it easier for them.

British Library Cataloguing in Publication Data

Branston, Peter
  Children and parents enjoying reading: a
  handbook for teachers.
  1. Reading (Elementary)   2. Reading –
  Parent participation
  I. Title   II. Provis, Mark
  372.4   LB1573

  ISBN 0 340 38592 8

First published 1986

Printed and bound in Great Britain for
Hodder and Stoughton Educational,
a division of Hodder and Stoughton Ltd,
Mill Road, Dunton Green, Sevenoaks, Kent,
by Page Bros (Norwich) Ltd

Typeset in Ehrhardt by
Macmillan India Ltd,
Bangalore 25.

Contents

Acknowledgments

The authors gratefully acknowledge the help of school staffs in West Glamorgan who have assisted in the production and testing of the materials in this book, particularly Gendros Primary School, Craigfelin Primary School, Hafod Primary School, St Thomas's Primary School, Godre'rgraig Primary School, Terrace Road Primary School and Trallwn Infant and Junior Schools.

Particular acknowledgment should be made to Phil Andrew who helped to shape the original Caper idea and to Lynda Edwards for her enthusiastic support right from the start.

The authors owe a debt of gratitude to the West Glamorgan Schools' Library and Resource Centre for their advice and support.

Finally, the authors and publishers would like to thank the following for providing illustrations for the book: Tony Hinwood of the Hinwood Library of Ideas, David Letissier of Graphic Books Ltd and Chartwell Illustrators Ltd.

Comments from parents on the Caper scheme

Introduction

This book has been written for teachers who would like to foster collaborative reading between children and parents. Because *Children and Parents Enjoying Reading* makes such an attractive acronym, the term *Caper* has been used to describe the scheme throughout.

Caper is not a kit or a pack, as such, but a very detailed and practical scheme used with dramatic effect in one Local Education Authority's schools. The scheme did not develop from the view that parents fail to help with their children's reading. In fact, research suggests that the majority of parents are already involved in just that process. Equally, it did not arise from a belief that children are failing to learn to read, or that reading standards are falling. Again, the facts point to quite the opposite conclusion. Reading standards have risen consistently in schools over the past thirty years and the overwhelming number of children do learn to read.

Caper bases itself on a set of quite different assumptions. The first of these is that very many parents give the 'wrong' kind of help, often based on their own experience of learning to read in schools – experience which is now largely out of date. Parents need guidance, which this scheme provides, on more effective ways of helping.

Following on from this, many parents and children experience reading together as an unpleasant and sometimes painful chore, almost like visiting the dentist, only without the anaesthetic! To these parents the central theme of Caper, which is how parents and children can enjoy reading together, comes as a welcome relief.

Thirdly, it is our experience that although parents, in the main, support their children's reading at home, the help given is often spasmodic and unsystematic. Advice to parents in the Caper scheme is to read with their children for not more than fifteen minutes at a specified time each day. Built into the scheme is a simple method of monitoring this activity through the Comment Booklet reproduced at the end of this book (pages 103–6).

Finally, the Caper programme is based firmly on the assumption that the best way of fostering any activity is through enjoyment. Teachers will be only too aware that teaching children the technical skills of reading is relatively straightforward. Unfortunately, too many children appear unable to sustain a reading habit once the basic skills have been mastered. Caper attempts to offset this very real problem by emphasising from the outset a primary association between reading and pleasure. Pleasure is provided in the scheme:

(i)   by ensuring success even for the least able reader;

(ii) by identifying any failure as a failure to find the right book;

(iii) by stressing to parents that the reaction or response a child makes to a book is more important than the number of pages read (put another way, the quality of the experience is more important in the scheme than other quantitative aspects);

(iv) by defining a successful joint reading experience at home as one where two people together interact with an author's intentional or unintentional meanings;

(v) by engaging a child fully in learning to choose books for this experience;

(vi) by its stress first on enjoyment and only later on gains in reading age;

(vii) by a firm avoidance of an association of Caper with homework or 'prep'.

In the Caper scheme the point is firmly made that teachers with their special training will be engaged in teaching those skills of reading required, for instance, in understanding instructional texts, or in higher order comprehension tasks. They will also be demonstrating how reading develops an understanding of self and the world outside. They will, in addition, be stimulating an interest in, and an appreciation of, the literary value of texts. Teachers of infant age children will, with a range of method, be providing pupils with the necessary skills to become independent readers. With its stress on *books as fun*, Caper engages parents' interest and enthusiasm and powerfully reinforces a positive commitment by children to reading.

Caper, therefore, gives solid back-up to the wider reading and language activities of the school.

You will notice as you read through the book that it contains a good deal of material intended for copying, and the authors and publishers would like to stress that you are free to photocopy the following pages: 23–25, 28, 32, 35–40, 55, 60–62, 64, 65, 67–70, 72–74, 76, 77, 80, 89, 90–93, 103–112, 114–121.

Caper

Caper began as a collaboration between the deputy headmaster and the remedial teacher in one primary school in West Glamorgan, South Wales. The deputy headmaster had attended a School Psychological Service in-service training course on 'The importance of parents listening to children read' (Edwards and Branston, 1979) whilst the remedial teacher felt that his limited role restricted the contribution that he might make to children's reading in the school as a whole.

The Caper began in the first year junior class. Parents of children in this class were invited by letter to a meeting to discuss 'the important subject of children's reading'. That initial meeting surprised the organisers; parents proved to be eager to help, anxious for advice, and ready to follow suggested guidelines for encouraging their children's reading.

It quickly became apparent that there was substantial hidden parental support for their children in school and that the demand was not restricted to one class alone. The project was discussed widely amongst parents and the organisers met with repeated requests for it to be extended to other classes in the school. Over a period of four months, as and when adequate resources became available, the Caper spread from first year infant to fourth year junior classes.

The growth of the scheme had been so unexpected that baseline data was only collected in first and second year junior classes. A brief summary of the progress of this initial pilot study was reported by Andrew and Provis (1983) and Provis and Andrew (1984). A more detailed evaluation of the project, particularly at first year junior school level was undertaken by Provis (1984).

Following on from this very successful pilot study, the experience gained from it was offered as an in-service course for headteachers, their deputies and one member of their staff. The course was held in the pilot study school and the participants were able to gain information at first hand from the project's originators.

In preparing for this course, the organisers reviewed their efforts to engage parents throughout the year. Initial overtures to parents had been stilted, formal and somewhat hesitant, but as increased contact between teachers and parents proved to be such an effective interaction the dialogue with parents became less formal and more confident. Imparting this kind of experience became the central focus of the course.

In the second year of Caper the project was extended to five new schools which had volunteered, following the in-service training course. Each of the new schools began the project with six- to eight-year-olds. The staff engaged in the scheme met half termly to discuss difficulties and to develop and pool effective strategies for maintaining and sustaining the project. This in-service activity generated a great deal of teacher materials and resources which were collected together as a Resource Pack for Schools (Branston and Provis, 1984a). This pack proved useful for teachers within the project, who used it as a reference point, and for those considering such a project. It gave a clear indication of the scope and demands of the scheme.

'Reading Workshops' and 'Reading Clinics' were held for parents to help improve listening techniques. This material appeared as the Caper Workshop Pack and Caper Clinic Pack (Branston and Provis, 1984 b,c).

Much of this material is now combined into the present handbook.

By the summer of 1984 the project had been adopted in fourteen schools. Other schools eager to join were considering the scheme's requirements in terms of fiction stock and staff commitment.

The Caper Progress Report (Provis, 1983) summarised the gains made by the project in terms of:

1 Increased children's awareness of books as a source of pleasure.
2 Vastly increased children's book useage.
3 A readiness among even the youngest children to use the language of books – author, title, illustrator, and so on.
4 Gains in children's reading ages that reflected the reported level of their parents' involvement.
5 Increased parental involvement and support for a range of school activities.

The substantial reportage of subjective benefits deriving from the project, and the enthusiasm of teachers for continuation and further expansion of the scheme, were considered to be testimony to its success.

The Caper now belongs to the teachers who use it and who sustain their own enthusiasm for it by exchanging materials and resolving any difficulties collectively.

This book is not meant to be a simple description of Caper, but a practical handbook for any teacher who wishes to develop a parental involvement project with the parents of the children in their own class. The emphasis of Caper lies firmly in making reading at home a regular and *enjoyable* leisure activity. There are no 'pages set', there is no restriction on book choice. The success of the project hinges on good supportive adult listening to make reading 'fun'.

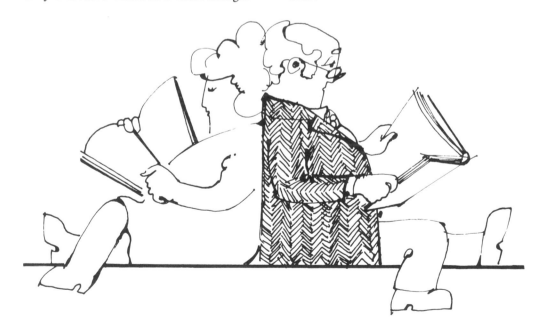

Setting out the aims of the Caper scheme

Any school intending to introduce Caper should begin by drawing up the aims of its scheme.

The project's aim should be clearly stated. Possible aims might include:

1 To promote the reading levels of children in school.
2 To foster positive attitudes towards reading.
3 To develop positive parental attitudes towards school.
4 To extend parents' and teachers' knowledge and experience of good children's literature.
5 To strengthen links between home and school.
6 To increase awareness of the essential parental contribution to the learning process.
7 To develop the connections between the reading process and other curricular areas, e.g. creative writing.
8 To extend one's knowledge and understanding of the reading process.

Wider discussion with colleagues and other professionals involving themselves in the project will result in a set of aims that reflect their priorities regarding the scheme.

The setting of aims is crucial, as a proper evaluation of the scheme's effect can only be made when outcomes are set against intentions. This will become clearer when the section on evaluation is read.

The Caper Calendar

WINTER TERM

Within 2 weeks	Prepare Comment Booklets; Prepare Flipsheets Hold an Evening Meeting for Parents
By end of September	Present Workshop 1
After half term	Issue Questionnaire 1
By mid November	Present Workshop 2 Organise in-school listening groups
By early December	Print new Comment Booklets Plan Newsletter Arrange Librarians' visit to school

SPRING TERM

At start of Term	Issue new Comment Booklets
End of week 2	Send Newsletter to parents
By mid February	Present Workshop 3
By half term	Visit to school by librarians
After half term	Offer individual clinic sessions
By end of February	Issue Questionnaire 2
By end of term	Present Workshop 4 Organise library visits for next term Plan Newsletter Print new Comment Booklets

SUMMER TERM

At start of term	*Issue new Comment Booklets*
End of week 2	*Send Newsletter to parents*
Up to half term	*Mount third series of individual clinic sessions*
During 5th week	*Mount Workshop 5* *Plan closing Newsletter*
At some point	*Organise class visit to local library*
Half term	*Newsletter to parents*

Questions teachers will want answered

What part do parents play in the scheme?

The part parents play in the scheme is spelt out clearly. Advice is given to them at an initial meeting, in the information Flipsheet (see pages 107–112), in the five parent workshops (pages 56–81), and in the individual parent reading clinics (pages 44–52). The bias in that advice is towards reading for meaning, minimising feelings of failure for the child (and, by implication, for the parent), and extracting the maximum fun from a book. Parents are steered firmly away from sub-skills training and the pitfalls of phonics. The underlying message to parents is that they are not to *teach* reading but to *demonstrate the fun* there is to be had from it.

Where do parents help?

The scheme assumes that parents help their children at home. Daily contact is established between home and school through the Comment Booklet (see page 103–6), which for children who are six and over is filled in daily by parents, but for younger children is completed once a week.

Schools will find that some parents are more enthusiastic than others and may wish to take a more active part in Caper. For those schools wishing to avail themselves of this extra support, the scheme suggests ways in which parents can help in school.

How much time does Caper take?

Teachers in the scheme look through every child's Comment Booklet each day and acknowledge each parent's comment. This takes no more than ten to fifteen minutes. There is a space in the booklet for the teacher to respond briefly to the parents at three weekly intervals.

What about all the other parts of the scheme?

The workshops and clinics are important but not vital parts of the scheme. They have been included in response to a demand from some schools for closer links with parents than are provided by the Comment Booklet.

The five workshops, one each half term (the scheme ends half way through the summer term), take approximately 45 minutes each. They are designed to reinforce the 'campaign' feeling of the scheme and will help to maintain its momentum.

The parent clinics run throughout the project. The aim is to see each parent listen to their child reading. Each parent and child session lasts for not more than 15 minutes. Teachers are advised that if resources do not allow all the activities in the scheme to be undertaken, their priority list should take the following into consideration:

Initial Parent Meeting: Essential, otherwise parents will not know what is expected of them.

Comment Booklet: Essential, providing daily feedback for the teacher.

Parent Workshops: These have proved very successful in reinforcing the Caper scheme; they are not essential, but add to the scheme's chances of success.

Clinic Sessions: Very important; the only chance parents will have of one-to-one practical advice. (If the choice is between parent workshops or clinics, give priority to the latter.)

What resources does Caper require, apart from time?

Caper cannot work without a plentiful supply of good children's literature. Details on this essential requirement are given between pages 20 and 21. At this point it is enough to say that children in the Caper scheme read a phenomenal number of books. A basic minimum of fifty books per class per half term is necessary for the scheme to get off the ground and to be maintained. An important challenge of the scheme is to beg, borrow or steal sufficient books for it to succeed. Advice is provided on the first and second of these! Most schools will have the reprographic equipment needed to produce the Comment Booklets, Flipsheets and other Caper materials arising from the project.

Will Caper interfere with the reading methods already in use in school or in class?

The short answer to this is a very firm 'No!' The stress Caper lays on the enjoyment of reading enables it to complement any reading method in school. Advice given to parents steers them away specifically from teaching reading, an activity which rests firmly with the class teacher. Caper's base in fiction and in reading for pleasure makes it unnecessary for parents in the scheme to become involved in the intricacies of instructional reading or of sub-skills training.

Children already take home books from the class reading scheme – does Caper interfere with this?

Caper co-exists quite happily with reading scheme books. A teacher may require a child to read a page or two from the class reading scheme as an exercise at home. Indeed this may sometimes be at the request of a parent. This activity can continue. The important addition is of fostering the pleasure to be gained from reading through Caper.

Will Caper work in just one classroom?

This book has been written precisely for the teacher who wishes to introduce the scheme in his or her classroom. It does work well even if only one teacher is using it. However, a 'two-class' start works even better because experience and resources can be shared. Furthermore, as will become apparent, at the evaluation stage of the scheme the results from two classes will be much more persuasive than the results from one.

Will Caper work with any group of children?

The materials in Caper were originally piloted with children between the ages of six and eight. However, it is now working successfully with pupils up to the age of eleven. It has been employed with older pupils who have experienced difficulty in learning to read. It is also being used in school in modified form with pupils of nursery and reception age – that is, between three and five. Pages 82 to 87 provide details of its application with this group.

While Caper works very effectively with less able children or with children whose reading development is delayed, it is advisable not to use the scheme *exclusively* with this group. It is all too easy in doing so to associate Caper with reading failure in parents' minds, which will create unnecessary problems if schools later decide to extend the scheme to other classes or pupils.

Does Caper work?

Caper very definitely does work. It gives parents the knowledge that they are helping their children constructively in their reading. It provides children with an extensive and early experience of good children's literature; it encourages the use of the language of books and fosters a positive commitment to reading. Caper persuades even the most reluctant reader that literacy is an attainable goal. Teachers involved in the scheme will find that, in explaining to parents how they contribute to the scheme, they will themselves become more sensitive to the processes of learning to read. Their understanding and knowledge of pupils is broadened as through their contact with parents they are made more aware of how pupils react and respond at home.

How can the scheme be evaluated?

Teachers will wish to evaluate Caper just as they would any classroom activity and precise methods for weighing up the scheme's pros and cons will be found between pages 94 and 96.

Two sorts of measure are suggested. The more subjective aspects of the scheme relate to changes in attitude which can be assessed using one of the Children's Attitude Scales and the Parental Questionnaire. Objective aspects, such as changes in reading age or number of books read, are easily measured. The evaluation can be used either to help the school decide to extend the scheme or provide information to the parents who have been involved in it.

The 'style' of the scheme

Caper will read as very prescriptive to some teachers, who may wish to make modifications to it. Clearly it will adapt easily without its central theme being lost. In our experience, however, teachers have welcomed Caper's precise structuring mainly because they have relatively little experience in working systematically with parents. Addressing a group of parents is recognised as a sometimes daunting task, quite different from that of standing in front of a class of children. Thus the 'model talks' to parents (see pages 26–32), which have been employed with a great deal of success, can, if a teacher wishes, be used verbatim.

Secondly, the campaigning style of the scheme may not appeal to everyone. Our experience, however, is that illustrated headings to letters, well-designed and frequent use of graphics, and a confident approach to parents help to promote an enthusiasm for the project which is an important ingredient in its success.

The research

Assumptions about the influence of the home

Large-scale studies over time, like those of Douglas (1964) and Davie *et al.* (1972), have all suggested that factors in the child's home affect performance in school. This has become an established truth in the minds of many involved with children and their education. Yet until the latter part of the 'seventies no one had been able to isolate any factor or group of factors within the home background of children that helped to explain their performance at school.

Many professionals have resisted the idea that schools play a relatively minor role in the development of children, or that parents are the key factor in their growth. In terms of time and opportunity to interact with children as individuals, the parent–child dyad is potentially more capable of providing stimulation and generating cognitive growth than the comparatively brief interludes a teacher can give to one child. The teacher may possess the skills but cannot spend the same amount of time in contact with the individual child that the parent can. The answer lies in getting parents and teachers to recognise this situation so that its potential can be fully maximised for the benefit of the child.

The vast majority of parents would help their children in support of their education if only they were offered some advice and guidance and ongoing encouragement. Teachers cannot expect parents to ask outright for such aid. The onus is on the school to initiate an appropriate dialogue.

The Plowden Report (Department of Education and Science, 1967) recommended as a minimum level of parent-school contact:

(i) a regular system of head and class teachers' meetings with parents before the child comes to school;

(ii) more private formal talks between head and parents, preferably twice a year;

(iii) open days to be held at a time when parents are likely to attend;

(iv) information booklets to be prepared so that parents are informed about the school and the manner of their child's education;

(v) written reports to be prepared at least once a year;

(vi) special efforts to be made to contact parents who did not take the opportunity to visit the school.

These activities may be commonplace now and have gone some way towards making schools less forbidding and more accessible to parents. However, these are all 'feedback' or one-way activities, which do not aim to engage parents in a sustained interaction with school.

In parallel with greater access to schools, there has been a growth in parental interest in children's education. The Bullock Report (Department of Education and Science, 1975) recognised the growing role of parents, but cautioned that whilst they were to be encouraged to borrow and buy children's books and to read them to their children, they were not to attempt to *teach* their children to read! This sentiment stemmed from a regard for the professional status of teachers and from concern that children should not be exposed to a multiplicity of approaches to learning to read. Nevertheless, any adult using a book with a child is conveying his or her concept of what reading means to that young child. Parents may not be consciously teaching the child to read, but learning of one sort or another is taking place.

Throughout the 'seventies the trend towards closer home-school links was continuing to spread, a fact highlighted by a National Foundation for Educational Research survey (Cyster *et al.*, 1980). This drew an 83% response from its target schools. The data collected indicated that:

> 95% of schools had a parents evening (half of these had a 75% + attendance);
> 90% made informal contact with parents;
> 65% sent out regular written information to parents;
> 90% invited new parents to visit the school;
> 35% of primary schools had a Parent-Teacher Association;
> 25% claimed they invited some parents to listen to children read.

This growing contact between schools and parents was noted in the Taylor Report (Department of Education and Science, 1977), where it was suggested that in the future a parent might

> 'communicate with his own child's teachers, in a spirit of partnership about the child's welfare and progress'.

The Report advocates partnership, not simply one way transmission of information from the school to the parent. The Report implied that the school had much to gain from such partnership, as

> 'both individually and collectively parents constitute a major source of support for the schools'.

Unfortunately the document failed to specify just *how* this relationship might be fostered.

Attitudes among parents

The Schools Council (1968) found that many parents, when asked about visiting their children's secondary school, reported a marked reluctance to make any contact. Typical remarks were:

> 'I never had to go there as there was no trouble.'
> 'I never had any complaint and knew the school were doing their best for him.'

The idea that no news is good news was frequently expressed, with many parents only expecting a dialogue with teachers where there was a problem.

The report drew three main conclusions:

1 Parents tended to delegate all the responsibilities for their children's education to the schools.
2 Some were reluctant to attend the school at any time, save by invitation.
3 Some who attended lacked confidence in their ability to have a satisfactory discussion with the teachers and expected a one-sided conversation.

In the same year, Young and McGeeney (1968), in a study of parental influence on children's learning, found a significant proportion of parents unwilling to 'interfere' in their children's education, whilst others were trying to teach their children using methods that often contradicted those of the school. Those who actively participated in teaching their children to read only did so to the point where their children could read at a very basic level, then felt their contribution was at an end. However, these researchers did find that parental interest, as evinced by their attendance at a meeting held to discuss reading, was closely linked to children's performance on tests of reading.

These two pieces of research suggested that parents' attitudes to school were often passive, but that positive parental interest in children's performance in school related significantly to educational progress. This poses the question: 'Can teachers help foster the positive contribution parents can make towards their children's educational development?'

Chazan *et al.* (1976) suggest that the attitude towards parents held by many teachers had tended to be somewhat negative, perhaps influenced by a perceived view of parents as apathetic or disinterested:

> Teachers can be discouraged by the apparent apathy and lack of understanding of the purposes of modern education of parents whose own educational level was low.

If this is the case, unless teachers act to break down this apparent lack of interest, there is a danger that a cumulative cycle of educational deprivation will be reinforced.

Schools might act to break into this cycle but as Chazan notes, there is much to be done in this direction:

> Little in the way of practical advice seemed to be given to parents in most areas and it is not surprising that the disadvantaged parents are unaware as to how to 'encourage' their child and so did very little that would be of any real benefit to the school.

It is this book's contention that the majority of parents are unaware of the scope of the impact that they can have on their children's school achievement, but that with positive guidance from school they are anxious and able to give support. Caper gives practical guidance on approaching parents and the necessary advice to enable them to give positive support in reading development.

A model from special education

Mittler and Mittler (1982) claim that parental involvement is more advanced and accepted in special than in mainstream schools. There seems to have been a greater awareness in special education that children's learning could

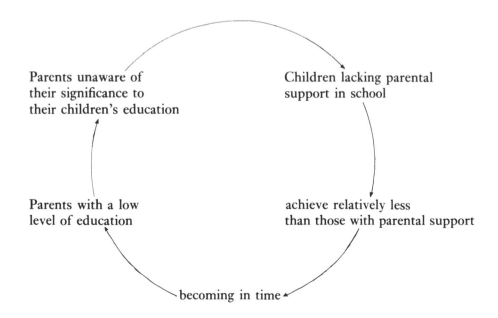

Parents unaware of their significance to their children's education

Children lacking parental support in school

Parents with a low level of education

achieve relatively less than those with parental support

becoming in time

only be fully understood as a function of environmental influences. The Mittlers' argument runs that, if home influences far outweigh those of school, it is essential that parents and teachers adopt common strategies and methods to maximise the learning experience of school. They write that schools have moved from a position of 'Keep out' through one of 'Come in!' to one of 'Please help!' This recognition of the parent's importance leads to a 'Consumer Model' of education: one in which teachers

'aim to augment parenting skills ... and do not try to change the consumer (i.e. the parent) into a professional teacher'.

The Caper scheme sees assistance with reading as one of these 'parenting skills' and one with which parents are only too ready to help if they can be given the right kind of practical advice.

However, presenting the model is not enough for, as Mittler and Mittler note, parents too experience very real difficulties in maintaining a collaborative partnership with schools. Many parents:

—have negative attitudes, arising from their own educational experiences;
—face the contrary demands of a busy family life;
—wrongly estimate their children's abilities (in special education this may mean under-estimate);
—attribute unrealistic levels of expertise to the professionals.

Caper attempts to break through these barriers to parental co-operation, by explaining how parents should help, by asking for a commitment from them of just ten minutes a day, by sensitising parents to their children's performance, and by encouraging parents' sense of significance to their children's success.

Changing parental attitudes

In 1975 the Department of Education and Science funded a study by Barbara Tizard, whose aim was to show

that the relationship between home and school could be changed in such a way that parents take a more active role than formerly the case in their children's education (Tizard, B., et al., 1981).

Five major outcomes were expected from such a change:

—the equalising of opportunity;
—influencing mother–child interaction so that no child was under-stimulated;
—increasing parental knowledge of education;
—promoting intervention in the first five years of life;
—altering the relationship of the schools with the communities they serve.

The study covered seven schools where the staff felt there was a potential for good teacher-parent contact, although, in the main, this was perceived as a one-way process in which teachers communicated their aims and methods but asked for little in exchange. This teacher-parent communication took the form of class prospectuses, newsletters, picture records, coffee mornings, parent evenings and weekly open sessions.

The project generated a range of 'two-way' activities which schools were able to mount. Some of the schools offered activities which involved parents in visits to toy shops, to public libraries, to holiday play centres and other centres of interest.

At the end of the first year of the study, between 30% and 68% of 'mothers' had been involved in more than half of the activities on offer. By the end of the second year this figure had risen to between 50% and 94%. A questionnaire survey of parents showed that generally more activities and still further involvement would be welcomed.

The researchers found some disparity between the perception of the parents and of the teachers as to which activities were the most beneficial. Parents tended to value those activities which emphasised the qualities of 'hard work', 'cleanliness', 'obedience', and the 'acquisition of established skills'. They often perceived activities which used materials such as sand and water as play, rather than experience-based learning. Any successful scheme of parental involvement needs to address itself to this potential mismatch between perceptions of education held by teachers and parents.

A year after the Tizard study had ended and the extra resources had been withdrawn, only one third of the activities had been curtailed. The activities which stopped were those that:

—required the borrowing of extra resources;
—were costly to run.

Again, any sustainable scheme should centre itself on activities with a low resource base, and should maintain close and frequent contact with parents to minimise the mismatch noted in other schemes.

Recent research into the relationship between background factors and pupils' achievement

Hewison (1979) attempted to discover whether demographic, cultural and attitudinal variables of home background were related to children's in-school achievement as shown by their reading attainment (reading attainment is considered to be the best predictor of subsequent educational success). She began with a pilot study in two infant schools and through domiciliary interviews in 65 homes obtained data on parental attitudes towards play, discipline, sharing activities, conversation, reading to children, children's leisure activities and attitudes towards school.

The factor that correlated most highly with children's reading attainment was mothers hearing their children read at home.

From this pilot study Hewison expanded her research to 107 children and their parents in four junior schools. Using a closed interview schedule, which she had devised from the pilot study, she explored the significance of a wide range of factors. The interview covered aspects of mother's language behaviour, her willingness

to 'chat' to the child in a variety of situations and her willingness to answer a variety of awkward questions! Hewison set this information against the child's performance on a reading test and an intelligence test. The results suggested that the relationship between Intelligence Quotient and reading attainment did not hold where children were 'coached' by their parents.

This study raised the question of what role the school might play in promoting reading at home. The data suggested that a high proportion of working-class parents spent time in coaching their children in the 'mechanics of reading', though none had consulted the school at any time, nor received any advice from school.

Can this support be enlarged and guided?

In collaboration with the late Jack Tizard and W. N. Schofield, Hewison set out to examine the causal relationship between parental help and reading performance. The research population was 1,867 six- to eight-year-olds from six multiracial Inner London schools (Tizard, J., et al., 1981).

All children in the project were given baseline tests. Two of the schools developed a parent involvement scheme, two of the schools were given an extra teacher each and two schools were used as control schools. The top infant class (six- to seven-year-olds) at each of the two parental involvement schools was selected as the target for intervention; the other classes at these schools formed within-school controls.

These target classes were allocated one research worker each, who gave frequent advice to parents and monitored the development of the project in the school.

Most parents welcomed the idea of the project, agreed to record their reading activity with their children, and accepted the idea of home visits. During these visits the research worker observed the parents listening to their children reading and then offered advice on good practice. In one school parents were asked to listen four times a week; in the other, parents were asked to listen three times a week, using scheme readers of comparable difficulty.

One class in each of the schools chosen to receive extra teacher help was allocated the services of an experienced teacher who worked four half-days per week. These teachers provided language activities for small groups of children. The project continued over a two-year period. Children's reading performance was reassessed at the end of Year 1 and Year 2.

By the end of Year 2 a marked difference was evident between the experimental and control groups. The difference between the 'extra teacher help' group and the control group was less marked. By comparing the relationship between performance levels at the beginning and end of the research, Tizard, J. *et al.* (1981) found that:

—initial reading performance was a good predictor of subsequent reading attainment;
—the effect of parental help was evident no matter what the initial performance.

After two years the researchers pooled the data from the four experimental schools and concluded:

> Parental help both reduced the proportion of failing readers and increased the proportion of able readers. The lack of significant effect for the 'extra teacher help' children appears most evident in the lowest attainment band.

The researchers could not allow for incidental help given by parents of the control group of children. However, at the end of the project the researchers felt that they could conclude that the parental involvement group of children had made remarkable gains in their reading and that it was possible to suggest that a causal relationship did exist between parental help and the children's progress.

The growth of reading projects

In the wake of the research of Jenny Hewison there have been a number of projects involving parents in children's reading in widely separated areas. Perhaps the most quoted examples are the Belfield Project and the Hackney scheme known as PACT.

The Belfield Project

The Belfield Project began in 1978, in a social priority community school in Rochdale where the children's average reading test scores were 5 to 10 points below the national mean. It focused on younger children (aged five). It was mounted from within the school's own resources, and the controls were the cohorts of children who had passed through the school before the project began.

Parents were invited to an initial meeting and told that their children would bring home a reading book each day with a card giving suggested reading for that night. The parents would then hear their child read, initial the card and write any appropriate comments. The card and the book would be returned to school the next day. The staff gave some broad advice as to how parents should listen to their children reading.

The scheme was introduced as an exciting new idea to gain the children's enthusiasm.

The progress of the scheme was monitored by interviews, surveys, reading tests and analysis of school records.

The success of the scheme has led to its extension to the older age range in the school, but in a modified form. Success is gauged in terms of children's improved confidence in their ability to read, closer parent-school relations and reading scores on standardised tests (Jackson and Hannon, 1981).

The PACT Project

The PACT scheme (Parents, Children and Teachers) began in 1979 in primary schools in Hackney, an area in the East End of London. Its evangelical aim was to 'spread ideas, find resources and take the message to the unconverted'.

PACT recognises three crucial elements in developing a successful scheme:

1 Schools need to find ways of making contact with parents.
2 Parents need advice on how to hear children read effectively.
3 The contact between parent and teacher must be maintained.

The PACT team generated such enthusiasm for the project that 34 out of 48 Hackney primary schools joined the project in its first four years. There are no precise rules as to how a school should initiate a PACT scheme. For schools seeking guidance there are PACT booklets and newsheets. Recently the PACT team has published a book reporting their experience (Griffiths and Hamilton, 1984).

The scale of this project has proved to be both testimony to the enthusiasm parents have for such home-school involvement and the value teachers attach to this involvement.

Some PACT schools have developed their project to cover the whole age range of children in the school. One such school, the London Fields Junior School, reports having 155 out of its 162 pupils taking part in the scheme. All the London Fields school staff acted as reading tutors, seeing groups of about a dozen children for twenty minutes or more each day. This time was used to monitor progress, respond to the comment sheets and prepare the next reading.

The headteacher felt that the project had effectively added to the strength of his teaching staff. He noted some problems presented by the project in his school:

1 The cost of good reading material, in sufficient quantity, was high.
2 Some parents were not in sympathy with

the reading approach suggested by the school.
3 The scheme proved to be time-consuming, with the remedial teacher spending the last two weeks of each term organising and monitoring the scheme.

These drawbacks were set against the gains made in the quantity and quality of books being read, with consequent gains anticipated in children's vocabulary, grammar and spelling.

The headteacher felt that the success of the scheme hinged upon the commitment of both the staff and the parents.

The Coventry Community Education Project (CEP)

Eight schools were chosen in areas of the City of Coventry deemed to be socially and economically disadvantaged. Seven hundred and sixty-five children were engaged in the project and baseline measures of their Reading Comprehension scores on the Hunter-Grundin Literacy Profiles were recorded. A 'parent involvement in reading programme' was then set up in each of the schools.

The schools chose different groups of children for involvement in the scheme, some choosing all children, others only those children with learning difficulties. Some schools operated the scheme at Junior level only, others initiated it from the reception class onward.

Parents were contacted by letter, or through an explanatory evening meeting, or by two short consecutive meetings straight after school. As well as schools sending home reading books and record cards, parents were offered a range of contacts with the schools, from social to educational events.

Preliminary results from the project suggest that the children's reading comprehension scores rose above those of the national average of schools matched for socio-economic status. Tests of spoken language amongst infants gave scores significantly higher than would normally be expected amongst socially disadvantaged children. Furthermore, the gains from the project were considered to include an improvement in the quality of the free writing of junior age children.

Anyone seeking further information should contact the project organisers directly. (See also Widlake and MacLeod, 1984.)

But the school already sends books home

Many teachers already send books home for the children in their class to read, and others will suggest that this has always been an ingredient in good school practice. However, Hannon and Cuckle (1984), in a survey of sixteen infant and first schools, found that staff thought parental involvement in the teaching of reading a good idea but that they stopped short of helping parents hear their own children read at home. Their findings are summarised in the table below.

Even though this is only a small-scale study it does cast doubt on claims that schools are already assisting children's reading at home through the provision of reading materials and support for the parents. In other words, structured schemes designed to promote parental involvement are very much required.

The future of parental involvement in schools

The Thomas Report (ILEA Committee on Primary Education, 1985), *Improving Primary Schools*, unequivocally supports parental involvement in children's education both in the class and the home. The Report accepts that a great deal of teacher-parent interaction takes place informally, but suggests that there is a need for a formal commitment to parental involvement in schools. To achieve this, schools have to be more open, accessible and welcoming.

The Caper project offers a good initial platform for both parents and teachers to explore the potential of a good home-school dialogue.

Parents asked to help within school are offered advice and guidance on the task that they undertake. If parents are being asked to help by involving themselves in their children's education at home, then the need for guidance is even greater. However, not all teachers are confident in dealing with parents, particularly groups of parents. Many teachers have had no training in dealing with parents and it has long been accepted that the necessary skills are acquired by on-the-job training from other experienced teachers.

Factors affecting use of school reading books at home
(Hannon and Cuckle, 1984)

Factor	Proportion of interviews	Number of teachers
Teacher acknowledges the importance of parental involvement	100	20
Head allows books to be sent home	85	17
Teacher allows books to be sent home	60	12
Teacher allows books home without expressing reservations	15	3
Whether teacher keeps some record of the use of books at home	10	2

A recent survey of Initial Training by Atkin and Bastiani (1985) showed that over half of post-graduate certificate of education students, and one in four students on longer courses, had no preparation for work with parents. There is a danger that many enthusiastic teachers will develop views on the potential for parental involvement, in the form of received wisdom from older, more experienced colleagues whose own contact with parents has been less than fruitful. Others might recognise the promise that such contact offers, yet feel reluctant to take the initiative and to be the innovator who breaks new ground in a school.

The success of parental involvement in reading projects has been widely reported, for example, by Friend (1983). However, perhaps the greatest argument in favour of parental involvement in children's reading is that it can secure about one hour's effective adult listening for each child each week. When this is set against the findings of Southgate et al.(1981) the need for extra adult listening help becomes obvious. In a survey of teachers working with first and second year junior school children, they found that teachers listen to children read:

— on average 20–40 minutes daily;
— occasionally for 60–100 minutes;
— on average for 2–3 minutes per child;
— occasionally as much as 15 minutes per child.

This pattern of teacher-listening may be different in the infant classes, but many teachers feel that, no matter how long they spend in listening to children read, there simply is not enough time to hear them read for long enough, often enough. Caper does not advocate that the teacher abdicates this responsibility by leaving it to the parent. It simply allows the teacher to use a little of his/her time each day to secure *extra* adult listening support for children.

The Caper Bookstock

It is essential that a plentiful supply of books is available in the classes where Caper is introduced.

How many books?

Each class should aim to have a stock of fifty books at any one time. Since fifty books will be quickly read by pupils in the class, books will need to be rotated between classes involved in the scheme. Hence there is a reduction in the overall resources required if more than one class in school is working with the scheme.

Which books are suitable?

Before the scheme starts each Caper class examines the books already available to decide which of these are suitable for use.

(i) It is important that books in Caper should not resemble reading scheme books in any shape or form. The reason for this is to avoid as far as possible any suggestion that children are involved in a race or competition. Parents often associate a reading scheme book with 'work', whereas Caper is firmly about reading for enjoyment.

(ii) To give the project the right kind of image in children's eyes, books chosen should be up to date. Apart from old and revered favourites, books which have been in the class library for much more than five years are unlikely to be suitable for the scheme. Similarly, old or dog-eared books should be avoided. They may, of course, be very *popular* books and up-to-date copies will need to be obtained.

The advice given to parents relates to one kind of reading, that is reading for pleasure. Caper books are therefore nearly always *fiction*. Non-fiction material requires quite a different range of reading strategies which do not fit easily into the Caper model.

'Easy' or 'hard' books

The aim of the scheme is to develop an early habit of regular reading. This can only be done if the books used, particularly at the beginning of the project, give children easy and ready success.

Caper tries to counter the strong sense very many children have that reading is a chore and mainly about getting through the reading scheme and then on to 'real' or 'library' books.

For many children the reading habit is not established through pleasure and consequently tends to die away especially as they proceed through secondary school. This is especially true of children who have not made a great success of reading early on. The bookstock should include plenty of good children's fiction which is easy to read. We need to begin to challenge the view commonly held by children and their parents that 'easy' books are necessarily babyish and therefore not worth consideration. Books by authors like Raymond Briggs, Pat Hutchins, John Burningham and Shirley Hughes suit this purpose admirably. The range of authors would also include those whose books require 'higher order' skills such as Roald Dahl and Helen Cresswell.

Getting to know books

Everyone in the scheme finds out more about children's fiction or about those books which do and do not work with children. Children's librarians are a mine of information in this respect. They can supply booklists and may well be willing to address parent or staff groups.

Every school in the scheme should obtain the following books, journals, or catalogues.

● *The Good Book Guide to Children's Books* by Bing Taylor and Peter Braithwaite (2nd edition, 1984: Penguin Books). This is an excellent book which provides short reviews under a range of headings. The fiction titles in *The Good Book Guide* are a must for Caper.

● *Books for Keeps*, published six times a year, from School Bookshop Association, 1 Effingham Road, Lee, London, SE12 8NZ.

● *Growing Point*, published six times a year, from Margery Fisher, Ashton Manor, Ashton, Northampton, NN7 2JL. This is a one-woman review magazine, well worth looking at.

● *Books for Your Children*, published four times a year, from Books for Your Children, 90 Gillhurst Road, Harborne, Birmingham, B17 8PA. This lively information magazine is written mainly for parents.

● *Signal: Approaches to Children's Books*, published three times a year, from Thimble Press, Lockwood, Station Road, South Woodchester, Stroud, Gloucestershire. GL5 5EQ. This is a critical review magazine.

Useful catalogues include *Puffin Catalogue*, Children's Marketing Department, Penguin Books Ltd, 536 Kings Road, London, SW10 OUH; and *Junior Paperback Catalogue*, Books for Students, 58/64 Berrington Road, Leamington Spa, Warwickshire, CV31 1NB.

Three excellent books which deserve a place in the staff library are:

● *Learning to Read with Picture Books* by Jill Bennett (2nd edition, 1982: Thimble Press)

● *Learning to Read* by Margaret Meek (1982: Bodley Head) – an extremely readable book for parents, which suggests titles for every age group, all of which are suitable for Caper.

● *Babies Need Books* by Dorothy Butler (1980: Bodley Head; 1982: Penguin Books) – an excellent book which parents and teachers will find very useful. It lists books for the 0–6 age group which should be available if Caper is introduced to Nursery or Reception classes.

Introducing parents to Caper

The project begins with an invitation to parents to attend a meeting on 'Children's Reading'. The invitation, like all Caper materials, should be eye-catching. Wherever possible the approach to parents should be made with humour and differ markedly from normal routine school letters. Experience has shown that the more stimulating the initial letter, the better the parental response. The average response to Caper has been near 90%, with never less than 70% of parents attending.

Naturally teachers know their own schools best and may prefer to devise a letter that will strike the right chord with their parents.

The invitation is sent to those parents whose children are in the classes participating in the project.

Invitation to the parents

Letter 1 (opposite) is sent to parents to assess their initial response to a Caper meeting. Please note that *all* letters and other project materials should be individualised for each school. Seek help with this from your local Schools' Resource Centre. If you are confident that most parents will attend a meeting, Letter 1 is not needed and you should start with *Letter 2*.
(*Note*: Experience suggests that Friday evening is a poor choice for a parents' meeting. Do not forget to fill in the name of the school in the drum (Letter 1) or box (Letters 2 and 3).)

Inevitably, some parents are unable to attend the initial meeting and a further meeting should be held just for them, using *Letter 3*. This attempts to draw in those parents who did not come to the first meeting by offering a more detailed invitation.

The tear-off slip on Letter 3 gives parents unable or unwilling to come to meetings the opportunity of individual interviews.

There will be a small number of parents who will not respond to these invitations. You may decide everything possible has been done to engage these parents in the scheme and accept that some parents will choose to remain outside the project.

Experience has shown that a telephone call or a home visit can act to stimulate the interest of this reluctant group. The question of home visiting is a delicate one and teachers who undertake home visits will be aware of the need to ask first, through the child, whether such a visit would be welcome.

The first meeting

The first meeting with a group of parents can be a considerable challenge for the teacher. The checklist on page 26 has proved useful:

Letter 1

Dear

We are drumming up interest in our own Parental Involvement in Reading Project.

If you would like to be involved with your child's reading development, please indicate below whether you would prefer to attend an afternoon or an evening meeting to hear more about the Scheme.

Yours sincerely

I would prefer to attend an   afternoon   meeting
                               evening

I cannot attend a meeting on a Monday/Tuesday/Wednesday/Thursday

Signed _____ Parent of _____

Letter 2

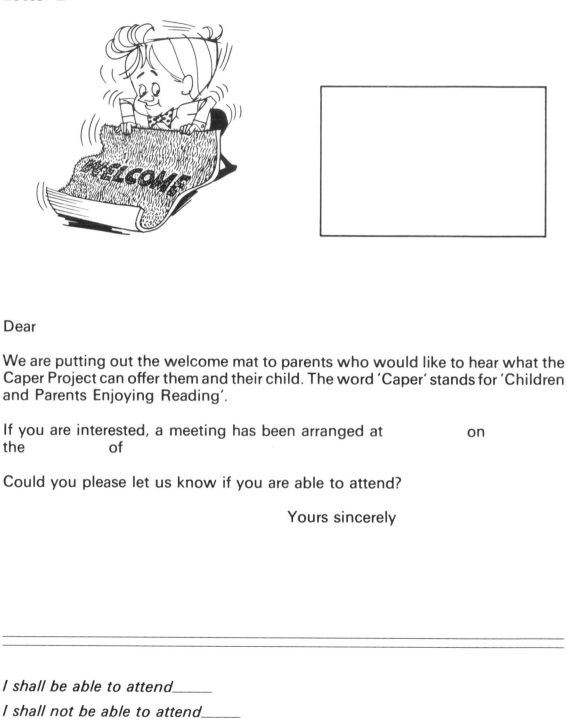

Dear

We are putting out the welcome mat to parents who would like to hear what the Caper Project can offer them and their child. The word 'Caper' stands for 'Children and Parents Enjoying Reading'.

If you are interested, a meeting has been arranged at   on the   of

Could you please let us know if you are able to attend?

Yours sincerely

_____

I shall be able to attend_____

I shall not be able to attend_____

Signed _____ Parent of _____

Letter 3

Dear

I was so sorry that you missed the reading meeting held at the school on   . For those parents who were unable to attend, we are holding a second meeting at

The purpose of this meeting is to explain how the school teaches reading, the importance of parental help in developing children's reading and how you can best help your child when he/she gets stuck on a word.

At this meeting all parents will be given a booklet entitled *Helping Your Child to Enjoy Reading*.

Please make a special effort to attend this daytime meeting.

Yours sincerely,

 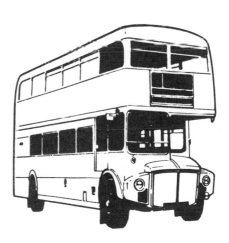

I shall be able to attend the meeting on _____
I would rather come another time _____

Signed _____ Parent of _____

1   If Letter 1 has been used, you will have some indications of the preferred times for meetings. The talk can be given at the start or the end of the school day, when some parents will be bringing or collecting their child. Evening meetings (avoid Fridays) are generally well attended.

2   The overhead projector and transparencies should be ready in advance.

3   Handouts, in sufficient numbers and appropriately personalised, should be ready for distribution at certain points during the talk.

4   Since reference is made in the talk to 'good children's literature', a display of this should be in evidence. An approach sometimes used is to distribute books to parents while latecomers arrive.

5   An attendance record should be kept to establish who is still to be contacted. A clipboard and pen should be circulated during the meeting.

6   Refreshments should be provided either at the beginning or end of the meeting. Refreshments demonstrate the school's commitment to the project and reinforce the school's welcome to parents.

Talking to parents

Two 'model talks', given to parents at an initial meeting, have been developed over the course of the Caper project. One talk begins by treating the parent group as a mock class, an approach which assumes a reasonably informal relationship between teacher and parent. Experience suggests that this style of presentation breaks the ice and encourages greater parental participation in the meeting and subsequently the project.

The second 'model talk' is recommended for use with parents of younger children (three- to five-year-olds) where the emphasis is on parents' skills of reading with, rather than listening to, children. This talk will be found in the section on Caper with nursery or reception aged pupils (pages 82–7).

Some teachers may not wish to use the talks in their present form. The talks have been included in this unashamedly prescriptive way for the following reasons:

—teachers, almost without exception, receive no formal training in working with parents (particularly in groups);

—teachers have little *experience* of working with groups of parents;

—as a result, we have found that teachers are often uncertain how to approach parents and what to say to them in groups;

—teachers and parents have responded favourably to the two 'model talks'.

By all means modify the talks or the presentations. It is important, however, to cover the central theme within each.

Model talk to parents of six- to eight-year-olds

1   *Headteacher's introduction (5–10 minutes)*

Opening ten minutes of introduction by the headteacher or the language specialist in the school, including an outline of the school's approach to the teaching of reading.

2   *Caper talk – Headteacher, classteacher or outside speaker – 40 minutes*

A light-hearted way to introduce the Caper is to address the parents as a class. 'Right, class, settle down!'

(a)   *Question session*

'Hands up all those parents of children in Mrs——'s class. Come along, quickly! This class is asleep today!

'Hands up those parents who used to read to their children regularly.

'I see, most of you – good.

'Hands up those parents who still read to their children regularly.

'Not quite so many.

'Hands up those parents who listen to their children read, at least every other day.

'Getting fewer.

'Hands up those parents who talk about the pictures in the book. A handful.

'Hands up those parents who talk about the story with their children.

'Hands up those parents who quickly say the word when their children get stuck.

'Hands up those parents who asked the school about their approach to reading.

'Hands up those parents who have asked the school what they can best do to help their children's reading.' (In practice this elimination game should have been won by the speaker long before the end; anyone left in the game is a saint!)

(b) *The research*

'We know that 60% of all parents help with their children's reading at some point in time. However, the research has shown that the most effective help parents can give their children, and one of the most important factors in children's reading development, is for the parents to listen to their children read aloud regularly at home. The purpose of this talk is to enlist your support in listening to your children read at home and to ensure that this support is consistent with the school's approach to reading and that you and your child enjoy reading together.'

(c) *The analogy with speech*

'Who taught your children to talk? How? You talked to them . . .

'Then you listened to *their efforts* at forming speech.

'Then you talked together.

'This process is still going on today. Apply this to reading with your child.

'Remember that even if your children are good readers, they are still only reading with the understanding, knowledge and insight of six- (seven-) (eight-) year-olds. Even very able young readers need the support and understanding of good listeners.'

(d) *How to listen to your child read*

Are you sitting comfortably?
Sit side by side so that you can both see the book easily, ideally in a room where there are no distractions, such as a TV set, or brothers and sisters.

Talk about the picture
Explore the picture on the page before your children begin reading. Ask them what is happening in the picture. You will find that they will often use the language of the book itself. In this way they will begin to anticipate the meaning of the print.

Talk about the story
Never recommence a story halfway through without reviewing the story up to that point. If you ended on, say, page 26 yesterday, do not just begin again on page 27 today, but get your child to retell the story so far in his/her own words.

What happens next?
Ask your children to predict the direction that the story will take so that they can compare their guesses with the story as the reading goes on. This tends to heighten their involvement with the tale.

Respond to the book.
Make your response to the difficulty level of books a flexible one; ask your child to read, but if the book is too

difficult, be prepared to share the reading or even to read it to him. If you do the reading, make sure that your child can follow the print and that you 'act' the story out with enthusiasm.

Another solution is that where the book is a little difficult for your child to read, be prepared to read the page first and then get him/her to read it after you. It is still reading; the reader's eyes are on the page, they scan the print and then say the words.

Try to remember that reading aloud is much harder than reading silently to yourself.

What do we do if they get stuck?
When children get stuck on a word, most parents ask them to 'sound it out' without realising just how difficult this is for the child. Try this. [Using the overhead projector, the speaker gets the parents to sound out the word, letter by letter.]

Never heard of it before – this is the creature you named . . .

You've all stretched the letters out to the point where they don't make sense. Asking children to sound out a word is often a mistake and the teaching of these 'phonic' skills is best left to the class teacher.

[If an overhead projector is not available, try the following as a group exercise.]

Sounding out is much more difficult for the child than we realise. What makes it hard for the child is that he or she cannot be certain of the sound value of each letter until s/he knows what the word actually says.

Someone reading with the child will know the word and therefore the sound value of each letter. If you know the word, phonics is easy; if you don't, it is very hard.

The teacher chooses a word (GEORGIE works very well) and write its *initial letter* on the board. The teacher knows the word, parents do not. The teacher asks parents to sound out the first letter. Usually parents will give soft 'G', hard 'G' and sometimes the name rather than the sound value. Encourage the class! 'Come on, you know this word. We had it yesterday!' (and so on).

Add the letters one by one – asking for 'sounding out' each time. Notice how often the group attempts to *guess*. The points to be drawn out are:

—confusion between sound and name of the letter even in experienced readers.
—difficulty of guessing sound values when the word is unknown.
—that a major source of irritation between learner and helper is involvement in a task together where one defines the task as 'hard', the other as 'easy'. (This is especially true where they are related, as anyone who has taught a husband or wife to drive will testify!)
—crucially for Caper, that this whole phonic exercise would have completely destroyed the flow of the story the child and parent were reading together.
—leave the teaching of phonics, if it is necessary, to the school.

The key to good supportive listening help is to look at your child to see if s/he is still scanning the print. If not . . . *say the word.*

It may be necessary for the listener to say the word two or three times in one listening session. Occasionally, it may be helpful to give the *first* sound of a word that has already been met several times in the text. If this results in your child trying to sound out every letter instead of reading the word, then it was a mistake that should not be repeated.

Perfect sense?
You are being involved in your children's leisure reading, so you should *not* attempt to correct every small mistake but accept those that do not affect the sense of the story. If you do this the story will flow, and your child will enjoy the experience and be prepared to repeat it.

When to listen?
Ideally you should attempt to listen to your child read every day, at a time convenient to you both, for a period of about ten minutes. Little and often is the key to successful listening.

Praise
Successful listeners praise their children frequently throughout each reading session for their effort at reading. (Many parents will wince at the mention of the red-faced table thumper who screams at the top of his or

her voice, 'I told you that before!') It is important that the tone of the session together be positive and that you act as a supportive listener, giving words of encouragement, 'good', 'well done', 'great', or simply sounds – 'Ah ha', 'Mmmmm'. Some parents find this extremely difficult, but it is crucial to successful listening.

If you notice that your children start to correct their own errors, it suggests that they are thinking about the meaning of what is being read, and you should adjust your listening accordingly.

(e) *Good practice*

At this point in the talk a school-made tape of 'good practice' is played to the parents to illustrate and reinforce the central points of the talk. This can be either an audio tape with the text displayed on an overhead projector, or a video tape.

It is a salutory experience for Caper teachers to tape themselves listening to children reading, and check that they can follow their own advice! To illustrate further the points in the talk, the 'class' can be offered a cloze exercise. Such an exercise should always reflect a contemporary theme. The passage below is part of a conversation between parents overheard in the corridor one afternoon

The parents are asked to offer the words that they used in the blanks. This has to be handled with some sensitivity, and care must be taken not to focus on anyone.

Questions to be asked

1 Did you 'sound out' the missing words?
2 Did you read up to the missing word and guess it?
3 Did you read beyond the missing word and guess back to it?
4 Did you have to use knowledge to find the word?

Strategies 2, 3 and 4 can all be used by young readers.

(f) *Summary of rubric*

The ideas raised by the talk are then reviewed by quickly running through the Flipsheet *Helping your Child to enjoy Reading*, which is distributed at this point. It is reproduced as pages 107–12 of this book and may be photocopied freely. (Users should not forget to add the name of their own school in the box on page 1 of the Flipsheet.)

● *What to read*
The parents are told that their children will constantly have a Caper book at home. These books will not be graded, as the children will have a free choice of book.

Cloze 1 For weeks now the _____ have been nagging at _____ to let them ____ and see the _____ Wars film called the _____ of the Jedi. I'm so fed up with _____ that I'll _____ give in and _____ them on _____ as it's their Dad's day _____. The _____ time we _____ to the _____ we saw a Disney _____. They still make _____ laugh. My _____ is Snow _____ and the _____ Dwarfs. I love the _____ called Doc.

The parents are asked to adjust their listening strategy according to the difficulty level of the book. This will give their children access to any book that they wish to read. (A short reading from a book such as *Not Now Bernard* by David McKee (Andersen Press; Sparrow), or a verse from Roald Dahl's *Revolting Rhymes* (Cape; Picture Puffin), will illustrate the fun to be had from contemporary children's books; plus the need for children to have access to such stories now, whatever their ages.) If a book is too hard, then parents are asked to read it to their children. If the book seems unsuitable, it should be returned to the school. *The message is that the fault lies with the book and not the child.* It is stressed that the books must always be read in *meaningful units* and not as *x* pages a day.

Parents are cautioned that listening sessions are more effective if they end whilst interest is still high. Ten minutes is quite long enough. Parents who find longer sessions successful may continue with them provided they are not pressurising the child.

● *How to use the Comment Booklet*
This is introduced as the pivotal point of contact with the class teacher. Having committed themselves to listening to their children read, the parents are asked to make a short comment in the daily comment booklet. This booklet *must* be returned to school each morning. The child will bring the comment booklet home each afternoon.

● *The programme of Clinics and Workshops*
The talk closes with the speaker outlining the programme of clinics and workshops. This provides the opportunity to secure the parents' commitment to attending future Caper events.

(g) *Questions and answers*

Many parents take the chance to welcome the project. Some will have held off rather than conflict with the school's approach to reading. Others may relate experiences that highlight points made by the talk.
Suggested answers to some questions which may be raised are given below.

Question: Is reading comics a bad thing?

Answer: Any reading material your child enjoys should be encouraged and this includes comics.

Question: My child reads very fast. He seems to gabble at words. Is this a bad thing?

Answer: Try to slow him down if he does not understand what he reads.

Question: My child seems to guess a great deal. Is this a good thing?

Answer: We all 'guess' when we read, sometimes incorrectly. [Show the illustration on page 32 on the overhead projector for two seconds.]

If you look carefully at the first caption you will see that 'the' has been written twice. In the second caption, 'in' has been written twice. People

often miss out the extra word because they are reading for meaning – and so they should! They are guessing what should be there. We mustn't try to stop children guessing.

But do try and encourage your child to guess sensibly. Do this by reading the sentence with the word missed out. You could ask: 'What word might fit in?'

Question: My child is a good reader, but he is not *interested* in books. What do I do?

Answer: The simple answer is, all children can be interested in books.

The challenge is to find the right books and then read them to the child.

Question: How much time do I need to spend on books?

Answer: This depends on the child. The answer is to make sessions regular. Better five minutes each day than half an hour once a week.

(h) *Drawing the threads together – the contract*

To sum up, the convenor of the meeting might say something like this:

'You've heard about the research and about the contribution you can make. The school is now committed to parental involvement in promoting children's reading.

'In essence you are asked to share a book with your child for ten minutes a day. You are asked to make a daily comment on your child's reading and to ensure that the booklet supplied comes back to school each day.

'You will have the opportunity to participate in twice-termly Caper Workshop sessions and to attend a termly Caper Reading Clinic.

'For our part, we shall offer a wide range of children's literature, advice and guidance to parents who want to participate fully in the project and the prospect of significant gains in your child's reading abilities. Thank you all for coming . . . '

Caper in the classroom

First meeting with staff

If a school is introducing Caper, even to one class, it is vital that a full pre-scheme staff meeting is held. Everyone then has an insight into the scheme. It is suggested that this meeting could be addressed by the teacher(s) who wish to introduce Caper to their classrooms.

At this meeting the contribution made by the class teachers to the project is outlined. The three main requests made of staff are that they share:

(i) a belief in the potential of the project, or at least an open mind about it. (It has been demonstrated that an optimistic view of the potential of the project is crucial to its success.)
(ii) a willingness to present the Caper as 'fun' and as an exciting bonus for the children. (It is *not* homework!)
(iii) a readiness to adjust classroom routine to accommodate the Caper and maintain the home-school link, through the Comment Booklet.

One should refer to sensitivities and anxieties parents may have in the school setting, and the differences between 'helping' and 'teaching'. It needs to be stressed that the extent of parent involvement is very much up to the school.

The Caper Comment Booklet

This is the essential link between home and school. The children put their booklets in a tray in the Caper Corner of the classroom as they come in each day.

The teacher reviews and initials booklets when convenient. This takes about 10–15 minutes each day. Some teachers may have reservations about this time allocation, but it is a small price to pay for gaining one hour per week extra language activity for each child at home. At the end of the school day the teacher returns the booklets to the children, praising those who have had them filled in. (*Note*: the comment, 'Didn't read', is accepted.)

Every three weeks, the teacher makes a short comment back to the parents in the space provided. If some criticism has to be made it should be balanced by a positive statement, e.g. 'Your comments appear to have dried up . . . and after such a good start.' One effective comment to parents is: 'I do so enjoy your comments.'

The importance of this Daily Comment Booklet cannot be over-stated. It is crucial in sustaining the parents' interest. One Caper Mum, an ex-teacher, commented:

'I always thought I was a good Mum, reading aloud to my children and hearing them read regularly. I would have said I did so every day. It was only the Comment Booklet that showed me how often I had missed.'

(It is often the children who pressurise the parents into listening, once the project is established. If this starts to happen it is a sure sign that you are generating real enthusiasm amongst the children in your class.)

To protect the Comment Booklets, wallets can be issued to the children to carry the booklets between home and school.
These can be:

1 *plastic wallets*, from any major educational supplies company; these are fairly durable and waterproof and have the added advantage of conferring status on those children who are participating in the project.
2 *class-made wallets*, using folded, stapled card. These have the merit of being self-designed, and the class can illustrate them with some thematic drawings, e.g. bonfires, Christmas, pets, seasons, faces and so on. These need renewing every half term and thus provide fresh impetus for the project; they have been favoured by most Caper teachers.

Many parents are not aware of their children's reading ability, and cannot judge the difficulty level of books; this quickly becomes apparent in their daily comments. These problems are met by the teacher placing one of three 'guidance to parents bookmarks' into the Caper books each time they are changed (illustrated on page 35). These are made by the class teacher on card and covered with adhesive clear polythene. These bookmarks are particularly useful in the early weeks of the project with children whose parents have not heard them read for some time. After a while they become less important as parents tune in to their children's reading. Do not write page numbers on the bookmarks. Caper is not a race or a competition.

If the Caper is presented as something routine and mundane, then it will quickly lose momentum. For many children, the project provides the first chance they will have to read a whole 'real' book themselves. Hence the teacher must attempt to maximise the project's impact on the class.

All good teachers strive to engage their pupils' interest and enthusiasm and the following ideas are those which Caper teachers have found to be effective in doing this.

Individual activities

1 Allow the children to change books as they return them, but present such an opportunity as a reward or a treat. Changing Caper books should be an event for the child.
2 At an appropriate time, get the children to report on their Caper book – not on its level of difficulty, but on the content of the story.
3 As 'favourite books' emerge, devise a waiting list, to be mounted on the wall, to prevent any squabbling over whose turn comes next. Large queues will quickly form for books that children have found to be a good read.
4 Prepare Giant Picture Cloze from selected texts to use to introduce children to new books; examples are given on page 36. Children can either draw an appropriate picture in each space, or a selection of illustrations can be prepared by the teacher. These give the children a chance to sample a text in a light-hearted manner before committing themselves to taking the book home. The result is that children learn to judge the worth of a book not by its cover but by its content.
5 The following are a series of review activities that Caper teachers have used to give the children an opportunity to review a book that they are reading, or have read. It is important that these review sheets are not used as *work*.

Examples of review sheets will be found on pages 37–40.

**Guidance
bookmarks**

CAPER	CAPER	CAPER
Talk about the picture. Let your child read the story.	Talk about the picture. Share the reading.	Talk about the picture. Read the story to your child.

Give plenty of praise.

If stuck, say the word.

Please keep commenting.

Giant Picture Cloze examples

Mrs. Wobble The waitress

[   ] was a waitress. When she carried a [   ] it wobbled.

She wobbled a bowl of [   ] The soup landed on a [   ]

customer's [   ] It barked.   Then she wobbled with a roast

[   ] The chicken landed on a customer's best [   ] Her hat

was ruined. The [   ] sacked poor Mrs. Wobble. She went home to her

[   ] who tried to cheer her up.

The   ENORMOUS crocodile

The Enormous Crocodile crept over to a place
where there were a lot of coconut trees. He
knew that children from the town often came
here   looking for

[   ]

There were always some
coconuts on the ground that had fallen down.

The Enormous Crocodile
quickly collected all the coconuts that were
lying on the ground. He also gathered together
several fallen

[   ]

"Now for Clever Trick Number One"
he whispered to himself . "It won't be long before
I am eating the first part of my [   ] !

"Mister Magnolia"
by Quentin Blake

Mr Magnolia has only one [   ]

He has an old [   ] that goes rooty-tooty. And two

lovely sisters who play on the [   ]. But Mr Magnolia

has only one [   ]. In his pond live a [   ]

and a [   ] and a [   ] He has green [   ]

who pick holes in his suit. And some very fat [   ] who are learning to hoot.

He gives rides to his friends when he goes for a [   ]

Review Sheets examples

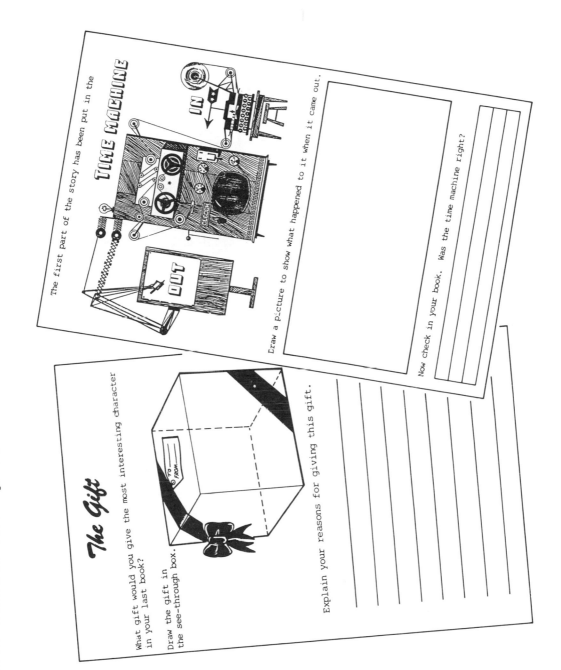

TIME MACHINE

The first part of the story has been put in the

IN

OUT

Draw a picture to show what happened to it when it came out.

Now check in your book. Was the time machine right?

The Gift

What gift would you give the most interesting character in your last book?

Draw the gift in the see-through box.

Explain your reasons for giving this gift.

Review Sheets examples

TELL YOUR FRIEND ABOUT YOUR LATEST BOOK

It was a feast of a book
Now tell the story in your own words.

And the saddest part was when

Review Sheets example

The
funniest part was

Colour the clown

RS9

Review Sheets example

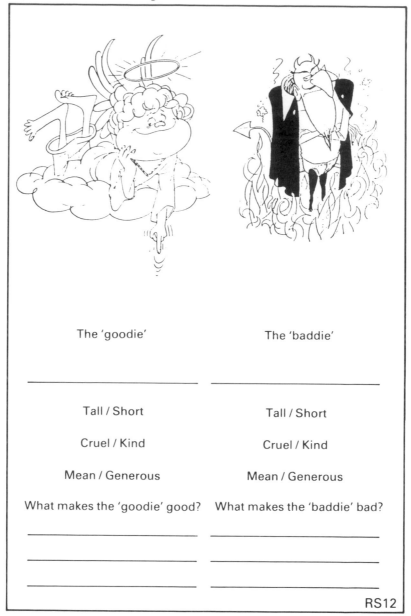

The 'goodie'   The 'baddie'

Tall / Short   Tall / Short

Cruel / Kind   Cruel / Kind

Mean / Generous   Mean / Generous

What makes the 'goodie' good?   What makes the 'baddie' bad?

RS12

Experienced teachers will have their own ideas that they have found useful in the past.

Group Activities

The following ideas are not necessarily a continuous part of the Caper Year but represent a range of activities than can be fed in from time to time to add to the momentum of the project.

1   *A daily review*
Teachers find that using the first fifteen minutes of class time to discuss the previous night's reading with the children forms a positive focal point for the Caper. During such discussion it is possible, even with 6–7

year old children, to talk in terms of author, title, illustrator, and so on.

2 *A shared review*
A group of four children is given the opportunity to read a book and then to present the group's views on it to the class as a whole.

3 *Choosing a book*
The teacher reads extracts from three or four books and asks the children which of the books they would most like to read and why. This helps children to realise that books are best chosen for their text, not for their covers.

4 *Theme readings*
The teacher introduces the idea of a theme to the class; this may mean anything from concrete concepts, like books about monsters, to more abstract themes, e.g. 'being lonely' stories. This is a very successful activity that gives recognition to the experience of books that the children have gained with their parents.

5 *Drama activities*
Items from a book that is particularly popular with the class can form the focus for a mime or even a scripted piece of dialogue. (Try *Not Now Bernard* by David McKee as a mime.)

6 *Percussive retelling*
Take a story, e.g. *Three Billy Goats Gruff*; by using clappers for goats one, two and three, a drum for the troll and a cacophony for the final splash, the narration can be effectively highlighted. This is a technique with which many infant teachers are fam-

iliar. No doubt the reader can think of many passages that lend themselves to this form of presentation.

Numbers!

Some Caper teachers expand the project into other areas of the curriculum.

1 *A straw poll*
Conduct a 'straw poll' of favourite books, authors, or types of books. Young children quickly learn to discuss books as true stories, animal tales, fantasies and so on.

2 *Block graphs*
Use the information from activity 1 to construct block graphs for display on the classroom wall. The children enjoy seeing how their preferences change over time and at the same time the graphs illustrate the children's expanding knowledge of books. It is interesting to note which old favourites remain popular throughout.

3 *Line graphs*
Example of the number of Caper booklets returned during the fourth week of every term . . . 'to see how well we are doing as a class'.

4 *A ratings chart*
Make a card index of all the books in the lending stock, then as the children finish a book they find the title in the cardex and put

their rating, from 1 to 5, of the book on the card.

1 = boring 5 = excellent

This helps children check if the book is rated a 'good read' by their friends.

Competitions

Many ideas are used by the Caper teachers to mount in-class book competitions, but the following competition is based upon a quiz that a Caper teacher set to maintain the momentum

ANNOUNCING A CAPER QUIZ

Try these six questions, and you could win the Caper Quiz. Use the local Library to help you.

1   Who wrote "The Magic Finger"? _____

2   Who draws animal pictures like the "Fishes", "Wild Animals", "Bears' Adventures", "Animal Homes"? _____

3   Name 2 Stanley Bagshaw books _____

_____

_____

4   Who wrote "The Three Robbers"? _____

5   Name 3 books by Maurice Sendak _____

_____

_____

6   Whom did Pat Hutchins wish "Happy Birthday"?

_____

Name: Class:

of the scheme during the holiday. The school offered three book prizes to the winners.
(*Note*: If you decide to set a quiz of your own, do consult the local Branch Library first as to the availability of the books concerned.)

Display

Caper teachers have used the following display ideas to add excitement to their classrooms.

—*Life-size favourite characters* (these are easily drawn by making acetate copies of the illustrations in books, then enlarging them using the overhead projector).

—*Frieze*, taken from the class 'book of the month'.
—*Comic strips*.
—*Murals*, e.g. from a scene in *Where the Wild Things Are* by Maurice Sendak (Bodley Head; Picture Puffin).
—*Character quiz*: which books do these characters come from (using illustrations and quotations from key figures in some favourite books)?
—*Collage* of a popular book to which every member of the class can make some contribution.
—*Posters* for the film of the book ('Now Showing', 'Final Week', 'Award Winner' and so on).
—*Giant scrap books* of favourite stories.
—*Zig-zag books*.

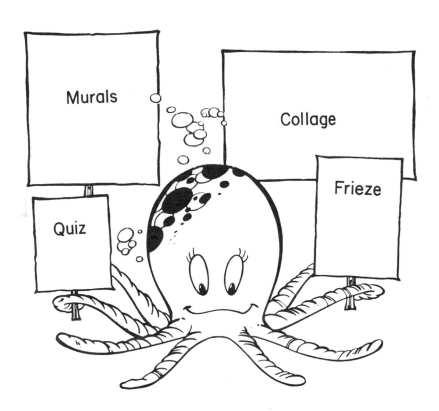

Parents within school

In the wake of the Taylor Report (Department of Education and Science, 1977), and the recent Government Green Paper (1984), greater, rather than lesser, parental access to school is likely in the future.

Caper sets out to involve parents in school in three ways:

1   as individuals, parents are invited to attend a termly Reading Clinic;
2   as large groups attending Workshops on reading, to discuss any problems the listeners are encountering;
3   as small groups timetabled to listen to children read, either within the classroom or in a library setting.

Reading clinics

Parents are invited to an individual clinic once a term. These sessions last, on average, fifteen minutes. They provide an opportunity for parents to:

(i)   demonstrate their listening skills;
(ii)   raise any questions about their children's reading;
(iii) broaden their listening skills;
(iv)   estimate general reading levels.

Many parents make excessive demands upon young children's reading and become frustrated when their children fail to meet these expectations. The results can be a battle over reading, leading parents to abandon what seems to be an uphill task.

The critical task is getting parents to be positive, interacting listeners who understand their children's efforts at reading.

These sessions help secure a full hour of good adult listening support for every child, each week of the project.

More than 80% of parents attended these clinics in the initial Caper schools, but do remember that the level of attendance will often be a reflection of the amount of enthusiasm the school shows for the scheme. Some parents need several invitations and considerable notice in order to be able to attend. The class teacher should send out the invitations four days before the clinic is to be held, then if anyone cannot make a particular time, further invitations can

Now, tell me the story in your own words.

be made so that there is a full list of parents to be seen. One way of dealing with this is to see one parent with her/his child at the close of afternoon school each day. In this way the parents of an entire class can be seen in one half term.

Timing the clinic session

If parents do not attend, then it is important to review the style of the school's approach; for example, it may be seen by parents as too threatening in tone. A ten to fifteen minute session provides a very limited chance for parents to exhibit their listening skills. The emphasis of the session is upon the parents' listening performance and *not* upon the child's reading skills.

Caution is necessary when giving advice, as reading is a topic on which parents often hold firm views. Their recall of their own reading development will often be imperfect. They often compress their own steady progress in reading into a sudden leap into fluency, and are unable fully to sympathise with their children and the problems they face. One can remember not being able to ride a bicycle and then being able to. We are looking at the area between these two states.

In asking parents to broaden their listening repertoire, the organiser should be prepared to *demonstrate* any technique that she or he discusses with them. It is essential that the advice be in the form of small changes in listening techniques and that no parent be overloaded.

The aim of these termly, one-to-one consultations is the *gradual development of good listening techniques.*

The organiser should advise parents that:

1. any new technique should be practised intermittently and not used during every listening session;
2. any difficulties in trying out new techniques should be reported to the teacher through the Daily Comment Booklet.

The teacher notes any advice offered to a parent during a clinic session and is thus well prepared for that parent's subsequent visits to school.

Organisation of clinics

The purpose of the clinic is to allow parents to demonstrate their listening skills and to raise any problems they may have encountered in listening to their children read.

The organiser aims to broaden their listening skills and to offer a supportive, sympathetic ear to parents in difficulty.

The list of topics dealt with in clinic sessions is substantial and only a limited number of the subjects raised by parents is covered here. The advice offered is simply an outline response as each Caper organiser will bring his or her own knowledge to bear upon situations as they arise. The suggestions in this section will be found very helpful in responding to parents' queries about *how* they should help, whether or not it is decided to organise structured 'clinics'.

In-school arrangements for clinics

Parents meet their children at the classroom prior to the clinic session. Each child has a favourite Caper book and a Comment Booklet to use in the session.

For every appointment, the organisers should make sure they have the name of the child and the *parent* beforehand. (*Note*: The parent's and the child's surname may not be the same – be aware of any sensitive areas ahead of time, if possible.) Reading is being portrayed as a shared experience, so the parent, child and teacher sit together alongside a table (*not* across the table from each other).

The parent and child begin by demonstrating how they share a book together at home. The use of a familiar, often 'easy' text reassures the child and results in a more representative reading performance.

The child is then asked to choose a book from a selection of slightly harder material. The choice of book is left to the child. This provides an opportunity to chat about reasons for choosing any one book. It may take three or four books to gain an adequate impression of a parent's listening skills.

Setting the right climate in the Clinic Session

At its worst, the experience of a child reading to his or her parent can be linked to a test or an examination.

One aim of the Caper is to bring the interaction to the point where a parent is willing to share in the fun of reading together, rather than approaching reading as a 'dour exercise in learning'.

The parent should understand that the purpose of the clinic is not to assess children's reading, or to examine parents as listeners, but rather to advise how parents might best support their children's reading. The teacher's role is advisory, not prescriptive.

In talking about books, handling books, and in listening to children read from books, the teacher must demonstrate his/her own enthusiasm for children's fiction and his/her awareness of the magic to be found in a good story. In every sense the organiser must present a good role model for parents, throughout each session.

Practical issues

(a) *When to listen*

Many parents are apt to listen to their children read at bedtime. Others set a definite time, e.g. six o'clock.

Experience suggests that whilst bedtime might be a good time to *share* a book, or to read a story to a child, it may not be the best time for young children to read.

Tired at the end of a busy day, their concentration may start to wander. Bedtime is often portrayed as an idyllic 'quiet time' whereas in reality it is a very busy part of the day. Children may quickly latch on to a ritual of *bedtime* reading which a parent cannot sustain.

The advice offered to parents has been to try to listen to their children at the same point during the evening, e.g. just after tea, rather than listening to them read last thing at night.

(b) *How much must we read?*

The saying 'little and often' covers this point. The Caper advocates that parents should listen to their children read for about ten minutes every night.

Parents are asked to end a listening session before the child's concentration starts to wander, or at least take over the reading themselves.

It is important to stress that all sessions should end at a meaningful point in the story, e.g. the end of a chapter or an incident, and *not* in mid-sentence or at the bottom of page. Stopping at a high interest point sustains enthusiasm (an allusion to the most recent episode of a soap opera helps to illustrate this).

(c) *Praise, how can I?*

Many parents report initial problems in setting the right tone for the reading sessions at home. They often speak of their own child's embarrassment and discomfort when she or he first encounters parents as supportive not critical listeners at home.

Sometimes this problem disappears as the child becomes used to the parent's new-found pleasure in his or her efforts at reading. If the problem persists, the teacher may have to negotiate between child and parent as to the most appropriate method of sharing a book together. A child may consider a particular phrase used by her mother as being childish and inappropriate now that she is in the top infants class!

This may seem trivial, but such hiccups can prove a real obstacle to effective listening, and to the parent and child getting maximum pleasure from their sessions together. Parents generally give insufficient praise. *It must be emphasised, however, that praise which is not sincere will quickly be seen as such.* The teacher should emphasise how well in fact the child is reading, by pointing to those skills which are being exercised and are passing unnoticed.

(d) *Talking about pictures*

Many parents find it difficult to talk about the story when they share a book with their children.

If the teacher senses that this is making it difficult for the child to read, then she or he must demonstrate how discussion of and questioning about the picture leads the child to saying many of the words in the adjacent text.

All parents are encouraged to use this approach but the 'picture–chat' approach is most relevant to the child who is struggling with a text that she or he finds demanding. If the organiser is confident that the child already utilises all the clues provided by the picture, then this advice may be superfluous, as the purpose of a good illustration is to encourage the flow of the story. It is *not* an opportunity to engage the child in some didactic diversion, e.g. 'How *many* trees?' or 'What colour is the dog?' Parents will need reminding that this is not some kind of teaching exercise.

(e) *Favourite and easy books*

Caper is attempting to develop a connection in children's minds between reading and pleasure. For this reason, plenty of easy-to-read books should be available. A book that is a 'good' book and easy to read

is likely to be enjoyed. Many children in Caper will, given a full choice, always choose a very simple text. In some cases this may even mean frequently choosing the same text.

Parents need to be reassured that children enjoy repeating successful experiences and that the re-reading of a favourite text is worth while. Parents should consider such favourites as possible presents. It may be that the child is playing safe with reading and is not yet ready to risk exposing himself or herself to making mistakes with more complex texts whilst the parent is listening. The clinic is an opportunity to demonstrate to the parent how much extra support is needed for young readers when they tackle more challenging material.

(f) *Guessing*

Many parents get distressed by their children's tendency to guess at unfamiliar words and familiar words in new contexts. They need to be reminded that guessing or predicting is *an absolute essential.*

It is important to enquire in detail about the nature of this 'guessing' and the manner in which the parent has responded to it in the past. If the guessing is completely wild and the word offered bears no relation to (a) the sense of the story, or (b) the initial letter sounds of the word in the text, then the parent may be leaving the child 'stuck' for too long. As a result, the child offers a word to fill the void rather than wait in silence for the listener's help. The solution is for the parent to give the correct word sooner.

If the guesses tend to correspond to the initial sounds of the given word in the text, then the parent praises the child for his or her effort and asks for a word that make sense.

'Good, you've begun with the right sound; can you think of a word that begins with that sound and makes sense in the story?'

This may seem a little cumbersome and should only be tried occasionally, but it does reinforce the value of guessing.

If the child's guessing tends to make *sense* within the context of the story, but bears little relation to the phonic structure of the word in the text, then parents must be cautioned against inhibiting such guessing. The teacher must indicate that without this skill of 'guessing for sense', the young reader would be ill-equipped to tackle an unknown text without adult listening support. Indeed rather than inhibit the flow of the story, the listener should accept the substituted word, provided the integrity of the story is maintained.

The listener may wish to return to the 'guessed word' at the end of the tale. However, such reviewing needs to be handled with sensitivity, e.g. 'That was a good guess, it made sense; the word is _____.'

Review initiated by the child (self-correction) is of course encouraged.

It may be necessary to demonstrate to the parent through a cloze activity (see Workshop session, page 66) that guessing is an essential element in reading. Indeed, to forbid a child to guess at print or, worse still, chastise him for it, will inhibit the development of fluent reading.

The child who has not learnt to guess without anxiety is generally reduced to inappropriate 'voice-pointing' or painful 'sounding-out'.

(g) *Pointing and voice pointing*

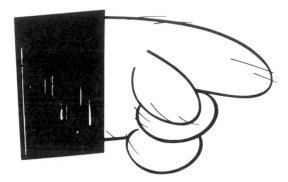

Many parents continue to point at words, or encourage their children to do so, long after it serves as a positive aid to reading. If this is the case, try to demonstrate that:

1 the child can read without pointing;
2 the pointing hand or ruler may be obscuring other information in the text that the child needs to generate the word he or she is stuck on.

Many children who read well regress to pointing if they begin reading more com-plex texts, or books with a smaller print size than they are used to. Their style of reading changes dramatically with changes in the nature of the text. Compare a child's reading of straightforward narra-tive with allusive or figurative texts (e.g. poetry), or with instructive material. A child's reading style cannot be judged from his or her approach to one text alone.

The problem of voice pointing (dis-jointed reading) is a common one. It stems from attempts to decode a word correctly as a simple isolated entity, sep-arated from its context. This may be the result of reading by pointing: the child's concept of reading is to voice in isolation the word indicated by the pointing finger.

It may help if the clinic teacher models the sentence that the child has just read and then asks the child to say it again in his (her) 'talking voice'. With luck, this offering of insight into reading may help towards the child's developing a more expressive reading voice. This process can be augmented by the parent using praise to punctuate the child's reading, thereby helping in the development of phrasing and expression.

(h) *'Stuck' strategies*

In the initial talk to parents, the emphasis is placed upon the parent saying the word

that the child is stuck on. This support should be early, consistent and kindly, in order to develop an enjoyable habit of parent and child hearing a book together.

Once this partnership is established, it may be possible to broaden the parents' listening approach.

(i) *First letter sounds*

By prompting with the first letter sound, the reader can then guess at the whole word.

However, if the result of such prompting is a laboured attempt to sound out the entire word and many subsequent words, then the strategy is counter-productive. The child has resorted to one restricted approach to print. In cases of very laboured reading of this kind, the book should be replaced sensitively by a book with a simpler narrative structure well supported by textual and visual cues and/or the helper should give prompter, more intensive support.

It is especially important for the child whose strategies have been restricted by a particular book to be reminded in this way that different strategies are essential. The strategies a child uses are as much determined by the book as by anything else. Reading a *story* needs particular emphasis with such children.

(ii) *Read up to*

Where appropriate, the listener can suggest that the child re-reads up to the 'stuck' word. Often this gives the necessary cue to the reader, who carries on without undue interruption.

Again, the purpose of this activity is to help the child develop appropriate reading strategies. It is done once or perhaps twice in a session. More than this and the flow of the story is broken (e.g. 'Let's try that sentence again . . . ').

(iii) *Read on and guess back*

Similarly, the child can be encouraged to leave out the word he or she is stuck on, read on to the end of the sentence and guess back at the unknown word. By placing the missing word into a meaningful context, the reader may be able to incorporate the symbolic and semantic clues to generate the unknown word.

Many children develop these strategies for themselves. Others need to be shown that it is possible to discover the unknown word in this manner and that this is a commendable strategy. In giving such advice to parents the teacher makes it clear that these strategies are to be used selectively and with flexibility.

The philosophy of Caper, however, remains that of assisting the child to read a text as easily and with as much enjoyment as possible. If a child is struggling with a book, *change it*. This is the message that must be left with the parent.

(iv) *Clueing*

The listener can be shown how to 'clue' the child into the unknown word. For example, if the text reads: 'The horses had not eaten any food for five days; they were *starving*; where 'starving' is the unknown word, the question, 'How would you feel if you hadn't eaten for five days?' might produce an acceptable guess.

The merit of providing clues in this manner is that it encourages reading for meaning and the development of a child's repertoire of reading strategies. Again, this technique can only be employed on those occasions when the missing word lends itself to such an approach.

(i) *Exchanging roles*

The clinics show how parents perceive reading and include a great deal of parent-child interaction.

One Mum demonstrated how, once the ten minutes was up, she might occasionally re-read a paragraph that had caused confusion and ask her son to spot any mistakes that she made. Mother and son readily demonstrated this technique and the boy visibly relished the role of editor for his mother's reading.

Whilst this activity produces an unusual stress on reading for precision, not necessarily in the spirit of Caper, the fun element was very evident. Mother and child had evolved an effective habit of reading for pleasure, and this is arguably the key to successful collaboration.

Advice and guidance should always be balanced against the dangers of disrupting an effective parent-child interaction.

(j) *Observation*

Observing the child read, i.e. actually looking at him or her rather than at the text, is dealt with in the Workshop section. However, it can be developed in the clinic session. Watching a child's eye, head, or hand movement will indicate the strategies being employed by the young reader faced with an unfamiliar word, e.g. looking at the picture, reading back, reading forward, beginning to sound out the unknown word, and finally looking up at the helper.

The enabling helper should supply the unknown word just after the child begins to sound out the unknown word. Parents will need help on judging the best moment.

More Detailed Guidance

Further guidance may need to be offered to three broad groups of parents.

The first group consists of those who find it difficult to listen to their children read because of doubts about their *own* literacy. If these doubts are well founded then the parent may need to recruit another listener, or may adopt a more passive listening role. In such an instance the school's interest may trigger the parent to seek help from an Adult Literacy Group. Experience with such parents has been that overwhelmingly they underestimate their reading ability. It is suggested that the teacher tactfully explores the coping strategies these parents use to deal with the literacy demands of every-day life. It is important not to over-react to an admission of illiteracy, as the parents may feel they have divulged a secret they should have kept. Remember that the standard of an effective helper's reading does not have to be extraordinarily high. Once you can show such a parent *how* he or she can help, you will have two people at least in the family with a keen interest in the scheme, both of whose reading can grow together.

The second group consists of those parents who find it difficult to hear their children read because of the children's behaviour or learning problems. These problems, whether real or imagined, require a positive response from the school.

The third group consists of those parents who have failed to involve themselves in the scheme or have children whose reading is not progressing.

The very few intractable problems of this kind which arise will need more intensive help. Regular reviewing of the Comment Booklet will highlight who these parents are. The scheme claims to be able to help all parents to share their children's reading experiences.

Paired and Shadowed Reading

The techniques described so far have been found to assist parents in promoting their children's reading. Other, more specialised techniques, with which teachers should be familiar, are paired reading and shadowed or simultaneous reading. These techniques are reported in detail by Bushell *et al.* (1982) and Morgan and Lyon (1979).

In the authors' experience, both of these can be tricky and definitely need to be modelled. Unless one is crystal clear how they work, parents will become very confused, hence it is essential that the organiser practises them first.

Simultaneous/Shadowed Reading

This is called 'simultaneous reading' in the literature; however, the word 'shadowing' describes the technique more accurately.

In its simplest form, the child and adult begin reading aloud together. The parent is asked to read slightly behind the child so that the child attacks the first sound of every word.

The child attempts every word. The parent simply completes the word that the child gets stuck on, allowing the child to correct himself (herself) if a mistake has been made.

If in the sentence given the child could not read the word 'engine', then what effectively happens is shown below.

Child: 'The blue train stood behind the e. . ngine.'
Parent: 'The blue train stood behind the engine.'

The parent begins reading every word one sound behind the child. However, as the parent is reading naturally, with no undue stress upon the difficult words, he or she often completes the word at the same time as the child. The value of this is clearly shown when the child cannot say a word. The child begins the word by saying the first sound, and the parent's correct (but not correcting) prompt enables him to 'read' the unknown word while maintaining the flow of the story.

The value of the technique is that it can be used to help the parent adjust to the child's own pace when reading aloud. At the same time, the parent learns not to stress any particular word, so that the child never gains the impression that he or she is about to attempt the reading equivalent of Beecher's Brook.

Difficulties which may need to be dealt with in the approach are as follows:

(a) parents may be reading too quickly, out-pacing the child;
(b) parents can become stuck on this particular strategy to the exclusion of others;
(c) this strategy can give over–emphasis to words the child cannot decode;
(d) context guessing is minimised in this approach.

Advantages of the approach are:

(a) the ease with which books are read;
(b) the consequent reduction in pressure on the child.

It is necessary to stress the need to 'take time out' from the strategy to ensure the child is understanding what has been read, by talking about the story or its characters, for instance.

Once the teacher is confident that this approach is working well for both child and parent (usually this takes about two to four weeks), then consideration might be given to moving the partnership on to paired reading.

Paired Reading

This is a comparatively new technique which has emerged in the last four years or so. All the research has been in the form of small scale studies, lasting two or three months, yet reporting huge gains in terms of rapid progress on reading tests.

1 Parent and child begin reading together as in shadow reading.
2 When the child wishes to read on her own she squeezes or taps the listener's hand.
3 This signal 'knocks out' or 'shuts up' the listener.
4 As soon as the child reads even one word correctly, the listener praises her.
5 The child continues to read alone until she gets stuck or makes a mistake.
6 The listener says the correct word, allows the child to repeat it, then both begin to read together again as in shadowing. This support must be prompt, within one second, or the child is left embarrassed and uncomfortable, waiting for the unknown word.
7 As soon as the child is confident that she knows even one word, she squeezes the listener's hand again and takes over.

The principal advantage of paired reading is that it enables a child to take control of the reading interaction. This turns the traditional approach on its head, and is immediately very attractive to young readers. In this approach the parent is seen very much as a resource. It takes at least twenty minutes to coach parents in this listening technique, and it requires patience and an appreciation that it is the parents and

their discomfort with which the teacher has to deal.

The progress of the partnership is monitored at intervals of two to three weeks, and at a time when the technique seems to be operating properly the parent is encouraged to tolerate mistakes to see if the child can correct herself from the context of the story. When this occurs then the child is doubly praised as this represents an advanced reading skill.

Paired reading is arguably expensive in terms of the time needed to train individual parents. Nevertheless, once the technique has been mastered it works well. Paired reading:

(a) maximises the child's independent reading;
(b) removes any sense of failure;
(c) allows the child to attempt to read anything;
(d) involves the child as a 'partner' in the reading process.

The checklist on the next page can be sent home periodically to monitor progress in paired reading.

Experience has shown that it is difficult for parents to sustain their use of this technique. A realistic time limit of eight to ten weeks might be negotiated at the outset, then if the parent and child wish to continue with this approach they can do so, whilst those who are finding it hard going can revert to less demanding approaches without losing face. There is a growing literature on the use of more specialised techniques (e.g. Morgan and Lyon, 1979; Young and Tyre, 1983).

One warning: the more specialised the technique, the stronger will be the message, unwitting or witting, given to parents that there is something essentially mysterious about helping with reading. Nothing, of course, is further from the truth. It is vitally important to demonstrate in every way possible that helping with reading is easy and fun!

Finally, a few parents may use this session to introduce wider topics, perhaps personal problems. If this happens, the teacher can either provide a supportive listening ear, or can help

Suggested checklist if children are using paired reading approach

Name: _____   Date: _____

PARENTS' CHECKLIST

1   Are you and your child reading together?
Are you adjusting to the pace of your child?
Does your child attempt every word?
Do you allow the child enough time?

2   Does your child remember to knock/squeeze?
Do you respond to the child's knock/squeeze?
Is your child *praised* for this promptly?
Are you ignoring minor errors, as suggested?
Does reading together begin again when the child gets stuck?
Are you giving frequent praise?

General

Are you doing everything you can to make reading pleasant and enjoyable for both of you?

Please sign and return to class teacher   ————————————————————————

56

parents identify those organisations within the community equipped to help with their problems.

We're here to serve YOU

Caper Workshops

The scheme provides for five reading workshops: one during each half term throughout the year. They provide a forum where parents can raise any questions concerning their children's reading, and share their experience and difficulties in hearing children read. The discovery that similar problems have been or are being encountered by others helps to reduce anxiety and puts their own child's performance into perspective. Parents derive comfort and reassurance from sharing their difficulties with a supportive group.

If the workshops are to be held during the school day, many parents will bring younger children with them. To enhance the sense of welcome, have some toys available for these children. The presence of very young children gives the workshop organiser the opportunity to raise the point that some youngsters, when reading aloud, cannot tolerate distractions. The workshop organiser can comment upon how hard it must be with brothers and sisters around to give ten minutes a day to just one child at a time. Parents generally enjoy this recognition of

their efforts to help with children's reading within a busy family context.

The workshop items are laid out in five separate units, but there is no set order for the use of this material. The workshop ideas incorporate:

—the Caper approach to reading;
—items that enable parents to experience young readers' difficulties;
—guidance on the use of this material.

The material should be used flexibly as many parents will utilise the workshop setting to raise problems and questions about children's reading. The organiser has to be prepared to explore these questions fully, to maintain the integrity of the workshop session. It is important to collect views from anyone wishing to contribute and to respect these ideas even if they conflict with one's own. Everyone must have the chance to agree to disagree. If presented with questions that cannot be answered immediately, the organiser should offer to bring a reply to the next workshop session. Experience shows that parents welcome such candour and it is a strong element in maintaining rapport.

Each workshop consists of two or three activities and some related exercises. At the end of each workshop, parents are given an activity to try at home. This forms the introduction to the next workshop.

Workshops should not last for more than an hour and a quarter. One must not overload the parents! At the same time do not dawdle through activities. A brisk pace needs to be sustained.

Five games are described at the end of the section (pages 78–79). These are to be taken home as 'language games' for children. They also help to break the ice in a workshop session. The games are a novel way of making introductions, and once everyone is seen to be fallible, the initial tension lightens.

Whenever possible, tea and coffee should be provided for those attending as it enhances their sense of welcome to the school.

To generate the atmosphere in which parents are willing to expose their problems in listening to children reading, the workshop leader has to be accepting of what the parents say and tentative in his or her response. The leader should convey no certainties as to what is best for any child but suggest that due to his or her experience he or she can advise on a range of strategies to meet most problems.

Parents will have useful advice for each other and the leader must make it apparent that she or he too is prepared to learn from them. To promote success the leader must ensure that she or he draws equally from everyone in the room and that no small group or individual dominates proceedings.

The most successful workshops are held in a classroom or library setting. Some Caper schools only have a hall available for use, but a group of thirty parents, in a hall built for two hundred, feel insecure and uncomfortable.

Whenever possible a member of staff from another class attends the workshop. This ensures that the school's approach to reading is readily explained to the parents and any problems in operating the scheme can be dealt with. A big plus for having another member of staff attend is that it ensures the workshop does not spill over into a complaints session about the functioning of the school or the performance of any one teacher. If this occurs in the presence/absence of a member of staff, the workshop leader must close down that avenue of discussion, suggesting that all such questions be raised with the headteacher, as they lie outside the brief of the workshop. Having a second teacher present may also alert him or her to the potential of parental involvement in reading.

Outline workshop calendar

WORKSHOP	DATE
1	3 weeks after scheme starts
2	2 weeks after half term
3	2 weeks after the beginning of the Spring Term
4	2 weeks after Spring half term
5	2 weeks after the beginning of the Summer Term

Workshop 1

Purpose (i) To eliminate any early teething troubles.
(ii) A preliminary exploration of ideas about books.
(iii) To look at the way parents perceive the reading process.

Resources for each parent

(a) A Caper Book.
(b) A paper and a pencil for activity 3.
(c) A picture book (may be shared) and some lined paper.

Activity 1

The content of this first session is largely generated by the parents themselves. Questions are raised concerning the routine functioning of the project and the leader is able to offer guidance where there is any uncertainty.

Many parents will report that their children are eager to read aloud. The reasons for this will include:

(i) There is no pressure – children are readily told the word when they get stuck.
(ii) Children are now reading aloud to good supportive adult listeners.
(iii) Children are being alerted to the fun to be had in good books.

Activity 2

Give each parent a book from the Caper bookstock and allow everyone five minutes to examine it.

A discussion explores these questions:

1 Would this book be of interest to your child?
2 Can your child read this book independently?
3 Can your child read this book with you supplying the word she or he gets stuck on?

A diversity of views will arise on the difficulty and interest level of the books and parents' opinion of their children's reading ability.

Draw together the threads of the discussion, emphasising that many children's books are written with interest ages of five, six, seven and eight but a reading age of twelve years plus. (Are these books necessarily excluded?)

Then read some selected extracts to the parents to illustrate the dilemma, using, for example:
The Twits by Roald Dahl (Cape; Puffin Books);
How the Whale Became by Ted Hughes (Puffin Books);
The Wind in the Willows by Kenneth Grahame (Methuen).

The point is made again that these stories interest the children, but the children can only gain access to them with the help of an interested adult.

Activity 3

The framework of letters shown below is put on the overhead projector. Parents are issued with pencils and paper but asked not to write anything yet. The parents are asked to study the three groups of letters for about one minute; then the overhead projector is switched off and parents asked to copy out what they remember.

r	s	v	t	b	p
l	m	o	w	q	d

(after Clay, 1979)

Examine the parents' efforts at random and share their efforts with the group.

The results

—Most parents recall the top line.
—This line may not necessarily be presented in order.
—Many parents space the letters equidistant from each other instead of grouping them in blocks of four.

Points to be drawn from the discussion are these:

1 Adults tend to read the letters from left to right – that is, they read by habit not according to an instruction. This contrasts with the way young readers tackle the task.
2 There are limits to our short-term memory (few parents recall more than eight letters). In view of this it is not surprising that:

(a) children experience difficulties in making a phonic attack on long words;
(b) they quickly forget words that they have already encountered in their reading.

(*Note*: One parent memorised all twelve letters by making nonsense words out of them. This mnemonic technique formed the focus for further lively discussion.)

Home Activity

Sort parents into groups of four who live near one another and can swop books easily at home. Give each group a picture book – for example, one of the following:

Jan Ormerod's *Sunshine* (Puffin Books);
Brian Wildsmith's *The Trunk* (Oxford University Press);
The Circus (Oxford University Press);
Shirley Hughes' *Up and Up* (Bodley Head; Armada Picture Lions)

Parents take the books home and get their children to tell the story of the pictures. The parent act as scribes, 'printing' the stories their children tell.

Each parent is given a couple of sheets of lined paper to write out the story. They indicate page changes with numbers.

On completing the book, the parent passes it on to another member of the group. Completed stories are returned to the class teacher. These stories form material for the opening activity of Workshop 2.

Workshop 2

Purpose   (i)   To examine children's expressive skills.
        (ii) To examine the use of limited information in reading.
       (iii) To examine technical aspects of reading.
      (iv) To broaden the group's understanding of the reading process.

Resources
(a) Completed stories from Home Activity Workshop 1.
(b) Overhead transparencies of different type faces.
(c) Pencils and Activity Sheet 2 for everyone plus overhead transparency of 'Badger's Speech' (see page 62 for this).
(d) Roald Dahl's *Revolting Rhymes* – or a similar book.
(e) Home Activity Sheet 2.

Review of Home Activity

The workshop leader begins by thanking parents for their efforts and notes that some of the stories were small books in themselves!

Points to stress
—Children tell interesting, exciting stories, using a considerable vocabulary.
Illustrate these with readings from their stories.
—For the majority of young children there is a gulf between their expressive skills and their reading performance, the former being well in advance of the latter.
—Good adult listening support gives children access to stories that match their interests, thus maintaining their enthusiasm for books and reading (i.e. books *above* reading age).

Activity 1

Using the overhead projector, examine a range of type faces used in children's books (see the examples on page 60).
Points which will come up are likely to be these:

—the difference between one type face and another is often as great as between individual letters.
—there is a sudden jump in children's books from *large print picture books to small print stories with few illustrations.*
—some type faces and letter spacing inhibits children's efforts at reading.

The workshop leader explains that many children do not easily make the transition to novel reading. They need support whilst they gain confidence in reading novels.

Activity 2

Give parents Activity Sheet 2 (page 61) and allow them a few minutes to try Section 1. The result will probably be that few words are completed.

Now get the parents to try Section 2. The result will probably be a little better. The first letter of a word is more useful in generating the whole word than the middle letter.

Repeat Section 2 by asking the parents to look at the Activity Sheet while the passage from *Hare and Badger Go To Town* (page 62) is read from the overhead projector. The result should be that all the words are generated.

In discussion, note that the flow of the story plus the first letter of the word will generate the missing word.
(*Note*: It is important not to expose any one parent's efforts. Simply ask, 'Has anyone got a word that fits here?' Those parents lacking confidence and anxious about their child's reading need encouragement and support, not exposure. The parent who has 'forgotten his reading glasses' may be retaining personal dignity by concealing reading difficulties.)

Activity 3 (time permitting)

Introduce a reading from one of the Caper books. Try 'Jack and the Beanstalk' from Roald Dahl's *Revolting Rhymes*.

Ask the parents to speak the part of the giant. If another teacher is present she or he can read the part of Jack.

Activity Sheet 1 (Workshop 2)
Sample type faces

Rumble and ramble
In blackberry bramble
Billions of berries
For blackberry jamble

Ben was not very surprised to see that the bus driver was different, and so were all the passengers on the bus. Ben tried very hard not to stare at the lady with the long tail, or the man reading his newspaper with one eye, and nobody stared at him.

The next day, Mr Mib was too busy to worry about the witch. He helped to arrange plates of food, bottles and glasses. At seven o'clock, Mr Mib changed in his cubby-hole, and filled his sack with parcels.

This time, as she came near, the dog didn't snap. It looked at her suspiciously, as if it doubted her good intentions, but licked its lips and eyed the water eagerly. Rose held out the cup slowly, taking care not to startle it. It drank the cup dry, then looked at her in the way Baby looked when he expected more. Rose filled the cup again, and this time as it drank, she eased the noose of the snare undone. It slid to the path.

Activity Sheet 2 (Workshop 2)

1 Each dash represents a letter. Construct one word to fit the information given.

_ _ u _ _

_ _ _ _ e _ _ _ _

_ _ l _ _

_ _ u _ _

_ _ _ d _ _ _

(Allow a few minutes for this)

2 Now try these words.

f _ _ _ _ _ _ _ _

m _ _ _ _ _ _

t _ _ _

l _ _ _ _

p _ _ _ _ _ _

u _ _

Present this on an overhead transparency for Activity 2.

Badger's speech (Workshop 2)

'Sad case,' murmured Doctor Mole, who seemed to know Fox well. 'Chemical burns. Factories, you know. We get plenty of those.'

'What do animals want with f _ _ _ _ _ _ _ _?' Badger said.

He had been silent most of the m _ _ _ _ _ _ . 'Humans have nothing to teach us. We have gifts and skills that t _ _ _ can never match. Besides we're quiet and orderly; we l _ _ _ _ no mess; we bring up our children p _ _ _ _ _ _ _ . We don't eat humans; we don't use them as they u _ _ us, and we don't need their nasty inventions!'

From *Hare and Badger Go To Town* by Naomi Lewis and Tony Ross (Andersen Press).

Through this tale demonstrate that it is not enough for parents to read the part of the giant, but that they must *be* a giant, both loud and rumbling, to maximise the potential fun in the rhyme.

Stress this need to 'interact' with print throughout all readings in the workshops. Emphasise that, to awaken their children to books, parents must let themselves go when reading together. You can only ask them to do this by demonstrating clearly what you mean.

Home Activity

Distribute copies of Home Activity 2 (page 64) and ask parents to get their children to:

(i)   Shade all the vehicles in the picture with one colour crayon.
(ii) Read the sentences and complete the empty blanks.
(iii) Tell the story about the sports car. Again the parent acts as scribe.

Ask for this activity to be returned to the class teacher on completion.

Workshop 3

Purpose

(i)   To distinguish between expressive language and the often artificial language of reading primers.
(ii) To demonstrate the importance of illustrations.
(iii) To look critically at illustrations.

Resources

(a) Completed stories from the last Home Activity.
(b) Activity Sheet and a pencil for everyone present.
(c) Several series of books by different authors.
(d) Home Activity 3.

Review of Home Activity 2

Points to be made are these:

—Thanks for co-operation.
—All children can complete the sentences.
—This form of writing is very predictable and can be found in many of the old-fashioned reading schemes.
—Its purpose is to offer certainty and security to young readers and hence add to their sense of confidence.
—However, a perpetual diet of this vocabulary-controlled reading can prove boring, may frustrate young readers and ultimately alienate them from the world of books.
—The children's own stories about the motor car use ideas and a vocabulary that are not often found amongst 'learning to read' books. A gap exists between the simplistic language of many learning to read books and the complex expressive language of young readers.

Activity 1 – The Use of Pictures

The workshop leader asks, 'How many parents talk about the pictures with their children?'

Many parents express a reluctance to use the 'picture-chat approach' because they believe:

—their children should read straight away;
—their children do not want to bother with the pictures;
—valuable time is wasted in such talking.

Collect these views and then offer the following exercise (Activity Sheet 1) to demonstrate the importance of illustrations as a cue to understanding (page 65).
Fold Activity Sheet 1 along the dotted line and issue to parents with only the type face visible. Several parents are given the paper with the type face the wrong way up.

The leader says, 'Right, let's start reading together . . .' The leader then acts out the part of the irritable, harrassed adult listener.

'No wonder you can't read it you've got it upside down.'
'Come along you know *that* word.'

Home Activity 2 (Workshop 2)

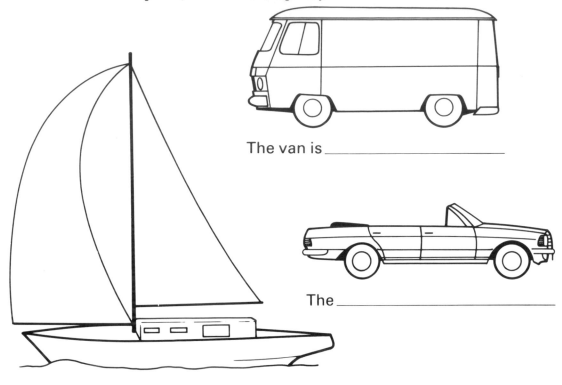

The van is _____

The _____

The boat is _____

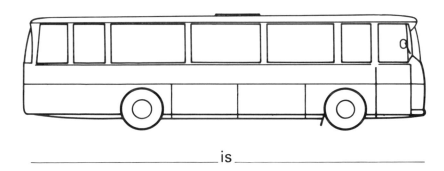

_____ is _____

_____

_____

_____

_____

_____

Activity Sheet 1 (Workshop 3)

⊡▽⊡ ∠▽⊓ ⊖∠ƨ ⏀▽↓↓.
"＞△□ƨ ▽~⊡ ∨↓▽⊓, ⊓▽↓↓⊓."
⊓▽↓↓⊓ ∠△↓⊡⊓ ⊖∠ƨ ⏀▽↓↓.
"○ ＞▽~ ∨↓▽⊓ ⏀▽↓↓ ⊡ƨ↓↓,"
⊓∠ƨ ⊓▽⊓⊓.

FOLD
- -

'But we had this yesterday.'

'I can't understand you; it's only a little word.'

Eventually the listener is reduced to an exasperated table-thumper, concluding, 'You do this sort of thing to me on purpose.'

This light-hearted presentation leaves parents eager to tell tales about the way they were heard read as children, and more importantly, the way they had listened to their children in the past.

The point is stressed that if readers cannot understand any word they must be given help.

At this point the page is opened up, and using the picture, the parents find that they can read the text. (Pencils will be of help here.)

Ask questions that lead the parents into reading:

—What is happening in the picture?
—Who is the man? Dad?
—What has he got? The ball?

Can you find any of these words on the first line?

Once parents are satisfied that they can read the text using the picture, spend a little time discussing questioning technique. This includes concrete questioning, like 'What colour is the toy?', and abstract empathetic ones, like 'How do you think the girl felt when her toy was broken?'

Distinguish between open-ended chat that allows children to explore the story and establish their own directions for it, and closed questions that lead the child towards verbalising the words that appear in the text below the picture. Emphasise that both forms of chat have immense value for children's language development and that neither style of questioning should be used exclusively.

Activity 2 – Picture-text relationship

Give parents the opportunity to examine a variety of Caper books and ask them to assess the extent to which the illustrations match the text. (A good idea is to give small groups of parents a series of books by one author.)

Parents offer their views to the group and the point is made that the use of the picture–chat approach depends upon the extent to which the picture relates to the text.

Home Activity 3 – Story sequencing

Use the four 'stories' illustrated on page 67–70. Reproduce them and cut each into the six episodes. Put in envelopes and hand parents one story each.

Ask the parents to take the pictures home and, through discussion, get their children to sort the pictures into a sequence that makes a coherent story. Discussions can begin by asking children to name the characters. Then they should be encouraged to tell the story from the pictures. Suggest to parents that they help children to expand the stories by asking, 'How did . . . . . . feel in the story?' Again, the parents scribe their children's efforts.

Encourage parents to swop envelopes, as there are four stories in all. They need scribe only one story each. Finished stories are sent back to the class teacher.

The stories illustrated here are most suitable for children of about six up to eight; at eight, more complete picture sequences may be required, and these can be found in Lesley Adamson's *I Can Write a Story* (Arnold-Wheaton).

Workshop 4

Purpose   (i)   To develop the picture text link.

          (ii)   To stress text and meaning links.

          (iii)   To examine non-verbal reading behaviour.

          (iv)   To examine reading for meaning through use of 'cloze'.

Home Activity 3 – story sequencing (Workshop 3)
Story 1

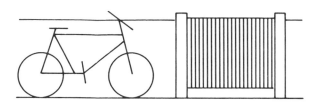

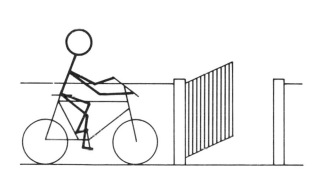
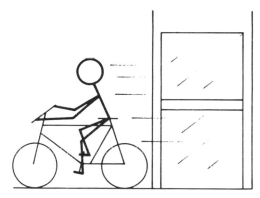

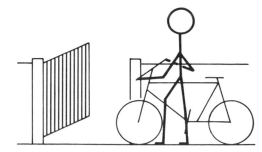

Home Activity 3 continued Story 2

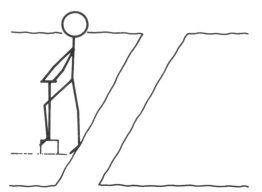
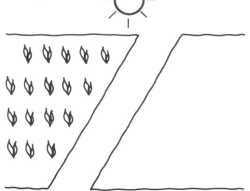

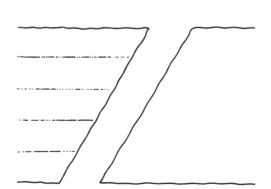

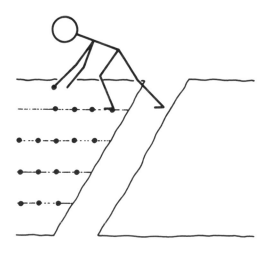
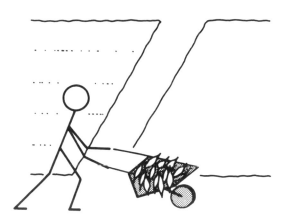

Home Activity 3 continued Story 3

 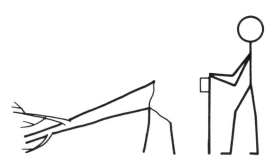

Home Activity 3 continued Story 4

Resources

(a) Completed examples of Home Activity 3.
(b) Activity Sheet 1 and a pencil for everyone.
(c) Activity Sheet 2.
(d) Overhead transparency of 'Insight Into Reading' (see page 74).
(e) Second copy of Activity Sheet 2 for use as a Home Activity.

Review of Home Activity

Read back some completed stories. Many parents will report that using the matchstick figures is a demanding task. Generally children enjoy the activity. It is interesting to note that many children make a perfectly viable, coherent story, using a sequence that differs from the original.

Activity 1 – Reading through knowledge

Issue Activity Sheet 1 (page 72) and a pencil to everyone. Give the parents a short time, one or two minutes, to study the 'signs'.

The teacher says, 'You have a minute to study these signs. Now turn over the paper and copy them out.'

At random, ask for any unusual responses, and with tact, use examples to illustrate key points.

(i) The task as a 'simple' learning exercise is too demanding – many parents will recall only two groups of words correctly.
(ii) Some parents use the list in a left to right sequence instead of vertically.
(iii) Many parents sort the signs to *make sense*.

ONE	WAY	STREET
MEN	AT	WORK

They read what they expect the text to say, given their background knowledge. (Is it parents who drive who sort the signs?)

Children do the same with words, i.e. they sort the text to make sense.

Activity 2

Pair the parents off and issue each pair with Activity Sheet 2 (page 73). Ask parent 1 in each partnership to complete each of the blanks in paragraph 1 with one word. Meanwhile, get parent 2 to observe the reader's face and not the text.

The teacher needs to be prompt in offering advice to anyone who gets stuck as this can be a stressful exercise.

When the majority of the group have completed the exercise, the parents reverse roles and attempt paragraph 2.

On completion, run through the cloze, asking parents for the words they put in the blanks. Accept all possible suggestions and then read the paragraphs in their entirety.

Ask the parents what they noticed as observers. Their comments may include:

1 left to right scanning;
2 hand and eye movement back and forth;
3 some 'talking out' of words.

The task of observing the reader is generally poorly performed due to a sense of mutual embarrassment. Emphasise that in observing their child's face they will learn a great deal about how he or she reads and when help is needed.

Use the following questions to raise some aspects of the reading process.

(a) Did you read the blanks straight away?
(b) Did you re-read up to the blank?
(c) Did you read on to the end of the sentence and guess back at the blank?
(d) Did you change your word in the light of subsequent reading?

Summarise these insights on the overhead projector, using the list printed on page 74.

Explain that these 'extra' skills supplement the advice given at the initial meeting for parents.

Activity Sheet 1 (Workshop 4)

Study the road signs below.

USE	AHEAD	STREET	MEN
SHOULDER	WAY	WAY	WORK
HARD	GIVE	ONE	AT

Activity Sheet 2 (Workshop 4)

Paragraph One

The _____ my eldest _____ started at the _____ school was one of

the _____ days of _____ life. She seemed excited _____ the

way _____ to the school, but once _____ the playground she

went _____ quiet.

The _____ rang so I _____ her to her _____ teacher. As soon

as _____ let _____ of her _____ she burst _____ tears.

I felt terrible, the _____ wanted _____ to _____ but I couldn't leave

_____ like _____ .

Paragraph Two

This Summer has _____ the _____ since 1976. It's the _____ time in

seven _____ that _____ have had a _____ sun _____ without even

_____ on holiday!

In fact, there were _____ when the _____ garden was _____ hot that

I could only _____ out for _____ brief spell at _____ time.

The _____ trouble was that the _____ all _____ up and _____ due

to _____ of water.

Activity Sheet 2 continued (Workshop 4)

Insight Into Reading

We guess at print	It is acceptable for children to guess.
We needed several attempts to get the unknown word.	Our children may need a little extra time to grasp the word.
We leave out unknown words and guess back at them.	Children may need to be shown that this is acceptable when reading.
We change our guesses in the light of further reading.	If children guess we need to encourage them to refine their guessing for sense.
For *us* the 'right word' is the one that makes sense.	If our children make sense of the text, but make an occasional error, we should not make them sacrifice the flow of the story for precision.

Home Activity

Give the parents a fresh copy of the cloze exercises to try on their partners at home, as this helps widen the reading awareness of all the listeners in the scheme.

Workshop 5

Purpose   (i)   To review reading for meaning.

          (ii)   To discuss 'islands of certainty' in reading.

          (iii) To explore the idea of comprehension and understanding.

          (iv) To discover the value parents place on Caper activities.

Resources

          (a) Overhead transparencies of three short, topical cloze passages (see instructions below, under Activity 1).

          (b) Activity Sheet 2.

          (c) Questionnaire.

Review of Home Activity

Read through the ideas raised by the cloze activity and attempt to reinforce the concepts of 'reading for meaning'.

Activity 1

On the overhead projector, get the parents to try three short, single paragraph cloze. Ideally these paragraphs should be taken from topical news items.

    Cloze 1 — with every 8th word deleted.
    Cloze 2 — with every 6th word deleted.
    Cloze 3 — with every 4th word deleted.

Run briskly through this activity and note that as adults have difficulty if the 'islands of certainty' get too small when reading, so do children.

Activity 2

Introduce the comprehension exercise on Activity Sheet 2 (see page 76). Use it as a straightforward exercise in English.

Read the passage aloud, with expression, then ask the parents to answer the eight questions underneath. They can note their answers, but there is no need to write full sentences, just notes to jog their memories.

Emphasise the fact that no one is to copy!

The result is that parents tend to answer the questions more or less correctly. They conclude that this shows they understand and comprehend the passage.

Accept their response and then introduce the two essay titles. Parents realise that it is possible to answer the comprehension correctly without knowing anything about it.

Discuss the need for effective listening with 'fluent readers'. Some children of six or seven can read texts with a language appropriate for children five or six years older than they are. However, there will be very few six-year-old children who have the comprehension skills of a twelve-year-old.

Even good readers need the attention of an interested adult to explore any ambiguities or uncertainties they experience when reading.

Activity 3

As part of a review of the year's events, issue the questionnaire on page 77 to parents.

Activity Sheet 2 (Workshop 5)

Comprehension

The Gribble strigged the blue black Dorigg into a drewish set of taygon. Shaking off the taygon the Dorigg frassed the Gribble with its mighty blawk.

In the end both the Gribble with its croving strigger and the blue black Dorigg were exhausted by the effort of it all. They embraced and agreed that it had been a good crimble.

1   What colour was the Dorigg?

2   What did the Gribble do to the Dorigg?

3   How did the Dorigg get rid of the taygon?

4   What did the Dorigg use to frass the gribble?

5   What word did the writer use to describe the Dorigg's strigger?

6   How did they both feel at the end of it all?

7   What did they do to make you think that they finished as friends?

8   Why do you think they thought it had been a good crimble?

Essay   Give a Gribble's eye view of the Dorigg.
Or   How would a Dorigg cope in a world without Gribbles?

Activity 3 (Workshop 5)
Questionnaire

Please tick those activities that you have tried this year.

First meeting   ———   Workshops   ———

Reading Clinics   ———   Library Event   ———

Bookshop Evening   ———

List the above activities in order, the most useful first, the least useful last.

——————————   ——————————

——————————   ——————————

——————————

Look at the following list of Caper materials. Give a score to each of them.
3 = very useful; 2 = quite useful; 1 = not of benefit.

Caper Flipsheet   *Helping your child to enjoy reading*   ———

Caper Comment Booklet   ———

Caper Newsletters   ———

Home Activity Sheets   ———

Caper Games   ———

Are there any activities you would like to see added to the Caper?

_____

_____

How many books do you think your child has read this year?   ——————

Which was the most successful book?   ——————————————

_____

Name of parent: _____

Parent of: _____

Workshop games

The following games can be used as 'warm up' activities for workshops. Anyone introducing these games into a workshop needs to have practised them beforehand.

Parents can use all these language games at home.

1 Going on a picnic

The group sits in a circle. The leader begins with, 'My name is _____.
I'm going on a picnic today. I'm taking _____.'

The item must begin with the same letter as the speaker's name.

> For example, *Mark* . . . a *melon*
> . . . *Marmite*
> sandwiches

The leader concludes, 'And I can join the picnic.'

Passing clockwise around the circle, each person gets the chance to state his or her name and the item he or she intends to bring.

If the person makes the name and item letter-link, then he (she) is told that he (she) can join the picnic. Those who do not make the link are told regretfully, 'You cannot come today.'

It usually takes two or three circuits before some of those taking part make the name-letter connection. By the end of the game each parent has been introduced to everyone else. Make sure the game ends before those left out of the picnic begin to feel uncomfortable. Never finish with a few anxious parents left outside the 'secret'.

2 Pass the buck

The 'Buck' can be a taped-up roll of heavy paper or a soft toy. The group sits in a circle.

The teacher explains: 'The Buck is passed around the group. If it comes to you, you must speak until I clap my hands. You then pass the Buck to anyone you can reach, in any direction. You must not throw it.'

This is an elimination game, i.e. anyone who dries up whilst they are holding the Buck loses a life. All players begin with three lives.

To begin with, make the speaking intervals very brief, but once the group has practised the game, vary the intervals and start eliminating the non-speakers.

At some point it may be necessary to introduce a 'no repetition' rule.

3 Random sentences

For this game you need one pack of letter cards. Each parent is given two small circles of paper to act as full stops. The aim is to create a sentence, however foolish.

The game moves clockwise. The opening player turns up a card from the pack on the table and says a word beginning with the letter on the card. The next player then turns up a card and has to say a word beginning with that letter which could conceivably fit with the first word, and so on round the table. The words must make sense! If a player gets stuck, he or she can use a full stop. Once the full stops have been used up, if players are stuck for a word, they are out of the game. Letters Q and Z are 'wild'.

It is a good idea to ask one parent to record the sentences so that they can be read back to the group at the end of the game.

4 Chinese whispers

The group sits in a circle.

The leader whispers a sentence into the ear of the person on his (her) left. The whisper is passed around the circle.

Once the whisper returns to the point of origin, retrace its course with each person stating what she or he heard.

Ask a parent to scribe the often hilarious results.
Ask someone else to begin the game again.

Close the session with a reading from *The Surprise Party* by Pat Hutchins (Picture Puffin), a book based on the same idea.

5 The preposition party

The group sits in a circle. The following prepositions are listed on the overhead projector or the board:

before	around
behind	over
beside	above
under	at
against	

Each player in turn begins a sentence with one of these prepositions.

The sentences must make sense in the context of the story. (Players are given three lives.)

This game is used with the last workshop of the Caper year as it is much more demanding than the others.

Listening groups

Once the scheme has gathered momentum, the parents can be approached for volunteers to form an in-school listening group. This further links the parents with the school and provides an excellent resource for the class teacher to draw on.

For the handful of children whose parents do not involve themselves in the Project, the listening group provides an extra in-school listening support.

The would-be volunteers are met as a group by the headteacher or the class teacher, who stresses the need for confidentiality concerning the reading performance of individual children.

To engage the parents in a successful listening group, it is emphasised that their commitment must be regular, reliable and sustained throughout the year. A small, sustained commitment is preferable to one which is inconsistent or erratic.

Those parents still interested in forming such a group are organised into a timetable, usually of hour-long sessions. One hour a day forms a realistic limit to enthusiastic listening and offers minimum disruption and maximum benefit to the class.

Sample listening timetable

A letter along the lines of the one given on page 80 should be sent to each parent in the group.

Notice that the contact point for making any adjustments to the timetable is in fact a parent, as this adds to the group's sense of responsibility.

To overcome any initial apprehensions, the parents should be given a short training session to reinforce the Caper message that reading is fun. They are asked to:

—accept the children's attempts at reading;
— convey their own sense of excitement and enthusiasm for the stories;
—praise the readers too much rather than too little.

A four stage model for listeners is then presented by the Caper teacher (see page 81).

Dear

As agreed, the Parents' Listening Timetable will begin each day at _____ and last for about one hour.

Please check that the information shown is correct.

Monday   *Tuesday*   *Wednesday*   *Thursday*   *Friday*

If there are any problems at any time, please contact _____ who will arrange a substitute for you.

Thanks once again for your support. We look forward to seeing you throughout the year.

Yours sincerely

Stage Model for Listeners

Stage 1

Where the young readers only know words they have seen in a familiar context.

Strategy: *Chat* about the picture with the child. *Say* the word, allow the child to *repeat* it, then *praise* his or her success.

Stage 2

Where the young readers guess at words from what they know about sentences, and do not relate sounds to letter shapes.

Strategy: *Give* the word; *read* the sentence; the child then *re-reads it*.

Stage 3

Where children seem to be uncertain about what the book says because of their own confusion of sound/letter relationships.

Strategy: *Say* the word or *clue* the word or *cue* the word.

Stage 4

Where the child is attempting to read for meaning and knows about letter/sound relationship. A child at this stage is developing his or her own cues and clues.

Strategy: *Re-read* up to the 'stuck' word, then miss it out and *read on* past the 'stuck' word to the end of the sentence. Ask the child to *guess* back at the missing word.

Parents need to be introduced gradually to this four-stage model until they can move freely between stages to adjust to each child.

There are many obvious limits to this model, but it forms a fairly concise starting point for the parents in the listening group. However, the best indicator of their success as listeners is the children's eagerness to take up the opportunity to read to them.

Parents can be engaged in listening within the classroom itself, or in a library area of the school. If the class teacher is thinking in terms of the former, consideration must be given to whether there is adequate floor space in the room and to the noise level generally attained by the class, as these may make the listening task too difficult to sustain.

If the library is the setting, then four or five well-spaced parent listeners at a time is a realistic number. The class teacher needs to meet this group about every half term to discuss any problems that emerge.

This high risk level of parental involvement has proved very successful in those schools which have developed it. Some parents have stayed on to help the teacher in successive years after their own child has moved on to another class.

Caper with nursery and reception age children

Caper was initially piloted with the parents of six- to eight-year-olds. It has also worked successfully with three- to five-year-old pupils, but the materials used and the advice given to parents has to be modified. This chapter has been written for teachers of Nursery and Infant groups wishing to initiate a Caper Scheme.

Initial Meeting with Parents

An invitation, using letters 1 and 2 (see pages 23 and 24), can be issued. Letter 3 (page 25) for those parents who missed the meeting should omit the reference in paragraph two to helping when a child 'gets stuck on a word'.

Attendance will be improved if, in addition to the letter, a poster advertising the meeting is displayed.

Parents are generally asked to stay on after they have delivered their children or to come in half an hour earlier. Space permitting, meetings can be held in one part of the classroom, while the children are in another part, supervised by the nursery assistant.

The 'model talk' for parents of this group of children has been written to engage children as well. It will, therefore, work just as well if parents and children are sitting together. (If only infant chairs are available, the speaker must be sure to use an infant-size chair as well.

Everyone quickly becomes accustomed to them.)

For this talk, an overhead projector and a supply of good children's books, suitable for this age group, should be available. As parents arrive, they should be given one of the books to look at.

Model talk for parents of three- to five-year-olds

Informal links between parents and teachers of this group of children are generally stronger than with older pupils. A formal introduction by the headteacher is, therefore, not regarded as quite as important to the scheme's initiation. However, a welcome by the head adds to the scheme's credibility and helps to establish it as an important new development in school.

Headteacher's introduction
(5 minutes)

(a) *The importance of reading:*

Academic and educational reasons:
Nearly all school subjects require an ability to read adequately; there is a very close relationship between reading and academic success.

The new and stimulating world of books:
Imagination, ability to think, to live happily and constructively, all are enhanced by the experience of books.

Crucial social skill:
As anyone who cannot read knows, we need to read labels, instructions, recipes, sign posts, even to watch television more effectively.

(b) *Can parents help?*

Of course. Parents can give the one-to-one attention just not possible in a large class.
There is a growing body of scientific evidence that parents can be, and are, of tremendous help in the reading process. It has to be the right help.
(*Note*: Prior reference to the earlier section on research (pages 11–19) will help in fielding questions.)

(c) *What is Caper?*

Caper is a simple scheme which helps you to help your child enjoy reading.
We are asking you to read with your child for about ten to fifteen minutes each evening.
(At this point introduce and explain the Caper materials and say how they are to be used.)

Books in the scheme:

A good supply of books is available. You and your child will select a book, take it home and read it together. Then you can change it.

Comment Booklet:

This is to be taken home by the parent and filled in each week, then brought back to school. The teacher will acknowledge it and make appropriate comments.

This record helps:

(i) to keep a written account of books read and the response of child and parent;
(ii) to foster the scheme;
(iii) to promote good home/school links.

(*Note*: Do not start the scheme immediately after the meeting. Hand out the Comment Booklets the following Monday and collect in the following Friday. It is worth stressing to parents that although the booklet is to be kept carefully—inside the reading book is a good place—it is not irreplaceable.)

Parent Workshops:

These are not as formal as in the scheme for six- to eight-year-olds. They represent an opportunity to gain feedback from parents and to suggest additional activities to them. Parent workshops need to be held every six weeks in order to maintain parental interest.
(*Note*: Individual clinic sessions are not felt to have a high priority with this age group. They may prove worth while with the one or two parents who fail to make the group meetings. It is also important to stress that any parent present at the initial meeting who wishes to be seen individually for advice or support needs only to ask. There may be some parents who are convinced their child is not progressing normally, or perhaps one or two who may lack the confidence to join in fully with the scheme.)

Class teacher's talk (20 minutes)

Aim: To give guidance on how parents should help children enjoy books.

Begin by projecting a cloze exercise on to a wall or screen. Any passage from a children's book will do, with one word in five deleted. The cloze passage on page 30, which was recorded in conversation with a parent, will work very well. Activity cloze on page 73 is equally effective.

84

Ask your group to read out the passage together as you point to each word. This is usually quite an amusing exercise as the group guesses at the missing words.

The purpose of the exercise is to demonstrate to parents that the processes they use when reading are very much like those used by children.

Central to the exercise is the importance of 'hypothesis making' in the development of reading (see Payton, 1984, especially Chapter 1 by Margaret M. Clark). The points to bring out therefore are these.

(a) *We guess when we are reading*
Children are listening and guessing as we read to them. They hear the beginning of the sentence. They often guess its ending before we read it, and *check* what we have read with their guess. Surprise comes when the check and the guess do not match. Encourage guessing by leaving out the *occasional* word for your child to 'fill in'.

(b) *Our guess is better if we can remember what we have just read*
Children's understanding is helped if we remind them *occasionally* of what has happened previously in the story. This is especially important in longer stories not finished in one sitting. (Refer here, if necessary, to serials or the weekly soap opera and the practice of 'recap'.)

(c) *Pointing at the words makes it more difficult to read with 'meaning'*
(If necessary, read again through the cloze passage, with exaggerated and delayed pointing at each word and deletion.) For young children, pointing is important because it focuses attention on words, helps develop the left to right rule of written language, and shows children there is a link between what is written. Children, however, respond to, and will have a good grasp of, the rhythms of language. Make sure you read to them with appropriate dramatic emphasis.

At this point in the talk, select two or three books to read to the group. Books that work very well for this exercise are *Jim and the Beanstalk* by Raymond Briggs (Puffin Books) (everyone knows the traditional tale, and this is an extremely funny sequel); *Rosie's Walk* by Pat Hutchins (Bodley Head); and *Peter's Chair* by Ezra Jack Keats (Bodley Head), a brilliant account of the jealousy caused by the arrival of a new baby and how it is resolved. Teachers will have their own favourites which will work equally well. Fourteen key points to be drawn from the selected reading are given below.

Key Points

(1) The most compelling part of a book is what happens next! In any book tensions set up are resolved in one way or another, although some books end on a further question mark – for example, 'the wicked wolf was never seen again ... for a long time.' Therefore there should not be too many interruptions or too much quizzing by the parent during the reading.

Begin by apologising for breaking this rule in the talk! You have to do this to illustrate the points you are going to make.

(2) Sitting comfortably

Make sure you and your child are sitting side by side so both of you can see the book.

(3)	When	Bedtime is *not* a good time. Children are usually tired. It is also a *busy* time of day. After tea, or when a younger baby has been put to bed, is better.
(4)	Children should become familiar with the 'language of books'	Give the title and author of the book. It is important to accustom children to the *language of books*, e.g. title, author, illustrator, chapter, 'dedicated to' and so on. These words should be introduced naturally as they arise.
(5)	Importance of illustrations	Allow parents to see illustrations as you read. (Not easily done. It requires you to read upside down!) Illustrations help children to understand what is happening or may happen in the story. Allow children to absorb the picture before reading the text. Do *not* use the illustrations to 'teach' ('What colour are the trees?' or 'How many boats can you see?'). This spoils the flow of the story and, of course, children's enjoyment of it.
(6)	The importance of 'cloze' or 'deletion' activity	As you read, stop at appropriate points and ask parents to supply a missing word. They can do this with their children, not to spoil the story or to turn reading into a too difficult quiz but to encourage guessing and prediction.
(7)	Active participation of the child	It is worth pointing out to parents too that inviting children to guess certain words will help to engage the child as an active participant. It encourages a child to interact with the text. Finally, and very importantly, it can tell a parent if the book is failing to interest.
(8)	Any failure is the book's and not the child's	At this point in the talk it is important to emphasise that just as adults may find a book is uninviting or boring, children often react in a similar way. If the child is unhappy with a book, the parent should change it, perhaps noting in the Comment Booklet *why* that particular book did not work (i.e. by asking the child). Caper is partly about children learning to choose books and making mistakes is a crucial aspect of this learning process.
(9)	Prediction	After reading a page or two of the book, ask the group what they think will happen in the story. Examine the clues in the text or in the illustrations which might have helped them in this prediction.

(10) 'Cloze' becomes easier for the group as the book comes to an end	Point out to parents how quickly they have learned to do the deletion exercise. You have engaged them in the story through it. The same process occurs with their children.
(11) Predicting the end of the story	When you arrive at the last page of the book, ask parents to guess the ending. This allows them to check with their earlier prediction. In some stories the ending may just be a 'one liner' – for example, in *Where the Wild Things Are* 'and it was still hot!'
(12) Response to the story	Ask for responses. Did the parents like it? Was it funny/sad or what else? Why did the group like it? Encourage parents to ask for a similar response from their children. These joint responses can be recorded in the Caper Comment Booklet.
(13) 'Easy' books are *not* boring	Ask parents whether they were surprised that such an easy book could be so engaging and whether they think their child would enjoy it.
(14) Retelling the story. Teachers who wish to know more about this should read *Story at Home and School* by Barrie Wade (1984)	Children will very often, quite spontaneously retell stories which have been read to them. They should be encouraged to do this. Retelling stories has a very positive effect on children's language development.

At this point, and if there is time, read another of the books to the parents. It may not have been possible in the first reading to bring out all the above points.

It is worth while bringing out some of the less obvious aspects of stories chosen: for example, in *Rosie's Walk* the fact that the fox is given no mention at all in the text, or that a common theme which children find intriguing is the journey or adventure which begins and ends at home. The talk ends with a recap of the points made in it. It is very helpful in doing so to produce a modified version of the Flipsheet (pages 107–112), taking out any references to hearing children read. The Flipsheet will remind parents of the scheme's purpose and will also give them support in explaining the scheme to other people at home unable to come. There may be some schools where parents might appropriately be asked to introduce the scheme to parents who did not attend. The Flipsheet helps them to do this.

Explain that as the scheme progresses further meetings will be arranged at approximately six-week intervals. The purpose of these has already been explained by the headteacher. It will be found that these subsequent meetings, here called 'workshops', are vital in maintaining the scheme's momentum.

For the nursery and reception class Caper, detailed workshop activities are not given. A formal approach to parents of younger children has not been found to be particularly successful.

However, the following activities work well: joint discussion of parents' comments in the Caper Comment Booklet, particularly about books that have worked and the reasons why they were successful; extending activities at home – for example, drawing pictures from books read; making up stories which parents record and bring to the group; reading poetry together; recommending and reading a favourite book to other parents. The list of activities is extensive and as parents meet further ideas will be suggested and can be followed up either at home or by the teacher in school.

The 'Caper Corner'

One issue relating specifically to Caper for the younger age group is how books are selected.

With this group, parents are invited into school to make the choice with their children. Most teachers will find this works best if the books to be borrowed are available close to, but not actually in, the classroom. This can be a corridor space, but it is all the better if a recessed area is available where parents and children can choose without feeling pressured. Books should, of course, be well displayed and not presented 'spine-on'. Again a good supply of books is an absolute must. The walls of the 'Caper Corner' can be used to display Caper-related activity, an up-to-date list of the top twenty books and so on. Parents are often willing to volunteer as 'library helpers'; one job might be to help with the wall display.

Caper Chain

These links are essential to maintain the momentum of the project whatever age-group is involved.

Newsletters

These perform the key function of reminding the parents that the project is an ongoing one and that they have made a commitment to it. They are best used at the beginning of a new term or just after half term, when some parents need to be restarted on the project.

The initial Caper Newsletters were factual summaries of the questionnaire results (see the section on Evaluation, page 94), and included some of the opinions parents had offered concerning the project (see Newsletter 1).

With experience these have become a little less formal, thanks to the use of Instant Art Graphics (see Newsletter 2). If you have no access to such resources, use children's illustrations to engender a brighter image.

Ideally, this form of reminder should be issued four or five times a year in order to keep parents informed of any developments in the project.

Graphics

If you have access to a Resource Centre, there is a large selection of 'instant graphics' which can be used to highlight any Newsletter or Information Sheet. These graphics can be photocopied and enlarged or reduced to fit any size of paper, up to A3. The lettering for the *Links* comes from a bank of Letraset instant lettering, examples of which appear below. The graphics and the lettering can be pasted-up to form a 'master' for photocopying or printing.

There is plenty of choice in LETTERING and GRAPHICS ☞☞☞

Newsletter 1

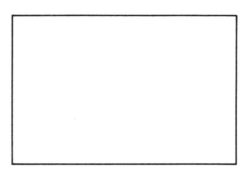

Dear Parent,

You have told us that _____ per cent of infant children now have a Caper book at home *every* day.

All of you listen to them read at least every other day.

More than _____ per cent of you said that your children are *eager* to read . . . this shows what successful listeners you have become.
Here are some of the things you said:
    'She now wants to read all the time.'
    'She is far more fluent in her reading now.'
    'He has really enjoyed the wide variety of books.'
    'He is reading far more than I ever thought he would.'
    'Reading has become part of our daily routine.'
    'He shows much more confidence in his reading now.'

There is now a completely new book supply in the classrooms and the children have new Comment Booklets.

Please keep up the good work and make sure you make a daily comment in your child's booklet.

If there are any problems, please call at the school any _____ day

Newsletter 2

Can you read?

animals can't read.

practice and improve!

exciting stories.

read them every night.

CAPER NEWS

I drew the line at hearing her read on New Year's Eve

If you cannot listen, please just make a comment telling us so in the Daily Comment Book

I've flown through more than 40 books since September.

This term the Children's Librarians will be visiting each of the Caper Classes to present a variety of book related activities.

This may be a storytelling session, a talk on favourite books and authors, a review of new children's books or a filmshow.

O.K. Nobody goes nowhere 'till I've read my Caper book.

Many parents have been amazed at the way in which their children have stuck to the task of reading aloud to them each day. This shows what good listeners these Mums, Dads and Grandparents are!

Newsletter graphics

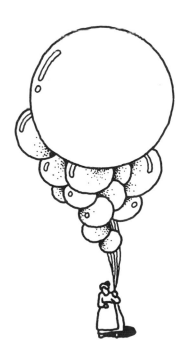

Memory joggers

Workshop graphics

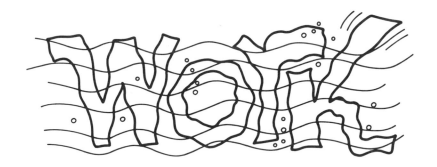

Evaluating the Caper scheme — has it worked?

Teachers will want to know whether the Caper scheme has been worthwhile, and will therefore wish to carry out some kind of evaluation.

Such an evaluation will help to decide:

—whether to continue with the scheme in one's class;

—whether the scheme could be introduced by other teachers in school, in particular those teachers to whom children already involved in the scheme will be moving the following September.

An evaluation of the scheme will give the feedback needed to tell if that extra effort demanded has paid off. Furthermore, an evaluation provides very useful information for parents. Teachers in Caper are urged to use a Newsletter, posters, or letters home to let parents know, as a group, how the scheme is progressing. This is a recognition of the vital role parents play in the scheme and the contribution they are making to it. Feedback to parents will help to maintain and develop the Caper scheme.

What is measured at the evaluation stage is determined almost entirely by the aims of the scheme, and readers will recall that the very first step in initiating Caper was to draw up, preferably with other teachers (why not parents as well?), the aims of their own school or class scheme.

Let us assume that the following were the aims selected. Alongside each aim, methods of measurement can be suggested as follows:

Aim	How to measure
To promote the reading levels of children involved in the scheme.	Assess the reading levels of children at the beginning and end of each year. Reading Quotients for project pupils should rise following the scheme. Reading Quotients are given in most reading tests. Otherwise they can be easily calculated using the following formula:

$$\frac{\text{Reading Age}}{\text{Chronological Age}} \times \frac{100}{1}$$

At the end of twelve months and without any kind of added intervention one usually finds that approximately one-third of a retested group have a Reading Quotient more or less the same, one-third a Reading Quotient higher than when first tested, and one-third a lower Reading Quotient.

This is simply the result of statistical variation.

Our experience with Caper suggests that two-thirds of pupils in the scheme have high Reading Quotients at the end of five terms than at the beginning.

Tests of reading vary. Most schools now use tests which assess Comprehension or Predictive skills as well as the more traditional 'word recognition' skills. Caper enhances both sets of skills, but particularly the former. Teachers can therefore expect particular gains in predictive and comprehension skills.

To promote language skills.	It is possible to obtain an objective measure of improvement in the area of language. The *British Picture Vocabulary Scale* measures the receptive vocabulary of $2\frac{1}{2}$–18 year olds, and is available from NFER-Nelson Publishing Company, Darville House, 2 Oxford Road East, Windsor, Berks., SL4 1BU. This test can be given at the beginning and at the end of the first year.
To foster positive attitudes towards reading.	This can be assessed on the basis of what children say about reading. Further checks can be made using one of the Children's Reading Attitude Scales printed on pages 117–21.
To develop positive parental attitudes towards school.	Check on this through the daily Comment Booklet, or in the parental questionnaires which can be found on pages 114–16. Do try to use these questionnaires or something like them. They provide invaluable feedback from parents and enable you in turn to let parents know as a group how Caper is going. You will be surprised and delighted by the feedback parents provide.
To extend parents' and teachers' knowledge and experience of good children's literature.	It is very simple to check on this. Note the increasingly knowledgeable remarks in the daily

Comment Booklet. It goes without saying that teachers who conscientiously check parents' comments will very quickly increase their knowledge of the books children read. Everyone involved in the Caper scheme finds out a great deal more about children's books.

To extend children's experience of books.

Check the number of books children are reading in a week or a month. Ask a colleague whose class is not yet involved in Caper to carry out a similar check.

Teachers have been astonished by the sheer volume of books children in the scheme get through.

Do not make the mistake of 'instructing' parents to 'hear page 26', or of using a page-number bookmark. This is much to much like home-work. *Caper is fun.* Children are, however, quite happy to keep a record of the books they read. Remember in checking the number of books read that Caper encourages the re-reading of favourite books.

As the project develops, teachers will notice particular incidents which may help other staff decide whether to embark upon Caper. These might include ideas for improving the approach to parents, a child's reaction to a particular book, or suggestions for the next parent Newsletter. It is suggested that each teacher in Caper keep a 'Critical Incident Diary'. This should not be used intensively, but simply to record important incidents which might other-wise be forgotten.

The Caper profiles give teachers an overall view of the pattern of Caper activity in their classrooms and provides a quick subjective means of reviewing the level of involvement of individual children.

Caper profiles

NAME	READING AGE SEPTEMBER	READING AGE JUNE	ATTITUDE TO * READING 1–5	NUMBER OF BOOKS READ	QUESTIONNAIRE 1 RETURNED	QUESTIONNAIRE 2 RETURNED	USE OF COMMENT BOOKLET 1–5†
Mark Hopkins	6.4	7.6	4	32	√	√	3
David Morgan	6.3	7.1	3	24	√	×	2
Lauren Hughes	5.9	7.1	4	27	√	√	5

* = 1 means never uses books unless told to
    5 means always in a book

† = 1 means comment booklet rarely returned
    5 means comment booklet always returned.

Conclusion

This is the only book we know of that gives down-to-earth and practical guidance on initiating and maintaining a parental involvement scheme in reading. Any class teacher can follow the plan set out and establish a successful scheme. The term CAPER was hit upon by the authors returning from a PACT conference in London. Caper reminds all involved that reading is first and foremost *fun*.

Caper is very firmly *not* about helping children to progress more rapidly through their class reading scheme. Unfortunately, and for a wide range of reasons, reading schemes are firmly established in parents' and children's minds as *work*.

Albert Hunt's very instructive essay 'The Tyranny of Subjects' (Hunt, 1972) describes the process whereby 'reading' as a total, holistic experience becomes redefined as a school subject. This process of redefinition begins at that point where children move from picture books to reading scheme primers. By the time the child has progressed through a set reading scheme the transformation is almost complete, and reading is perceived essentially as a 'tool skill' rather than an activity to be enjoyed for its own sake.

As the function of reading changes so the means used to teach it change. As teachers, parents and, therefore, children gradually modify their perceptions of the purposes of reading, so reading tends to be taught increasingly as a subject. Caper is attempting to re-emphasise to parents and children that books can be a source of fun, magic and mystery. Caper does not try to teach parents to teach but to help parents enjoy books with their children.

Some teachers make the cardinal error of using reading primers in the Caper scheme. Reading primers are used to *teach* reading and, as emphasised previously Caper does not teach parents to teach. Caper stands for enjoying reading. Therefore, it is very firmly based in children's fiction.

Caper defines reading as an interaction between a reader and the conscious or unconscious intentions of an author. It sees the reader as one who is constantly engaged in constructing meanings from texts. The parent's role in the process is simply to help the child make sense of what is being read. At no time in Caper is the parent asked to treat reading as a task, or to make that task more difficult for the child.

Parents are constantly reminded in the scheme that they should enjoy reading with their children, not treat reading as an obstacle race in which it is almost necessary to fail in order to succeed.

This requires constant reiteration because of the strong perception parents have that school is about *work* and work is necessarily unpleasant.

The vertical rise through reading primers unfortunately only serves to emphasise this perception. Try out the following reading perception questions with your class.

How many children agree with the following:

Agree   Disagree

Good children read hard books.

Easy books are books babies read.

I don't like reading 'easy' books.

You don't make mistakes when you read an easy book.

If you read an easy book you go on to a harder book.

Good readers read hard books and make mistakes.

Easy books are thin and hard books are thick.

Thin books are baby books. I like thick books.

Thick books are harder to read.

I like to read hard books.

Most six- to eight-year-olds reveal a strange pattern of responses to this test. A very significant proportion of pupils reject easy books that they can read in favour of hard books they have difficulty in reading. Similarly, they reject 'thin' books in favour of 'thick' books because they are being led to the view that the 'good' reader naturally gravitates towards the thicker book!

If there is an opportunity, refer to this tendency to assess books by weight when talking to parents about the last minute purchase of Christmas or birthday presents; this unfailingly strikes a chord.

Caper is unashamedly in favour of proving to children and their parents that books should be judged by their content not by their length or lexical difficulty. 'Easy' texts (and the word is in quotes because a book which is easy to decode need not necessarily lack complexity) are strongly recommended for Caper because they enable children to be and become readers.

An experienced reader appreciates reading as a qualitative experience. Caper attempts to encourage a similar response to reading in children. Therefore we do *not* count the number of pages a parent and child read together, but limit the session spent on reading to ten to fifteen minutes. Most teachers will appreciate the significance of what might seem a minor point. Counting pages emphasises a competitive element which does not sit well with enjoyment. A child and parent asked to read a number of pages will be conscious above all of fulfilling a quota. For some children, ten pages will seem very little; for others they may assume Tolstoyan proportions. A limit of ten to fifteen minutes makes the necessary allowance for individual differences. Furthermore, timed support is appreciated by parents who will know exactly what is expected of them.

It perhaps does not need mentioning that it would be a disastrous error to begin Caper by simply relying on a letter home without first having a parents' meeting. Anyone who even contemplates this is strongly advised to give Caper the widest berth. Caper will not work like this and in the long run alienates both parents and children. A proper introduction to Caper and its materials must start with a meeting with parents.

In this book we have attempted to give a class teacher all the information required to develop a parent involvement scheme in reading which we call Caper. By all means use this term, preceding it by the class or school's name. The structured materials, the letters and the model talks will help to get the scheme off the ground. This material can be modified as necessary so that it meets the needs of class or school more appropriately.

Once the scheme has begun, then of course one needs to maintain it, and the authors have provided in the text practical ideas to achieve this. Some of these may be thought to be too time-consuming. There is no doubt, however, of their value in developing and providing home-school links. The parent workshops and clinics, the newsletter and the parent questionnaires help to sustain parental interest and commitment. The in-class activities help to promote reading as a worthwhile activity in the child's minds. The books and the Comment Booklet sustain everyone!

Liaison, formal and informal, with other staff helps to sustain the scheme within the school. The evaluation which is a very important part of the scheme will help teachers and parents decide on the scheme's future.

Teachers using Caper need to be constantly looking out for books—a plentiful supply of good, easy-to-read children's fiction. A class of 30–35 pupils will need a book stock of 50 books per half term. This stock will then have to be changed or swopped every half term. For the five half terms of the scheme approximately 250 books are therefore required for the class. Do not be put off if there are not enough books or enough easy books to start with. Aim to build up the stock as the scheme goes on. We have suggested ways of doing this, either through borrowing books via a local resources or teachers' centre, through the children's librarians or through the school's Parent-Teacher Association. Another idea thought up by a teacher was to develop a book-sharing scheme in her class. Children bring their favourite books to school and are given an equivalent number of tickets. They then swop these tickets for books which other children have brought to school.

Remember—it is essential to have a good supply of books, but this can be built up relatively quickly.

Finally, the materials and ideas presented in this book have been generated, used and modified by Caper teachers in West Glamorgan. We should be very grateful to hear of the progress of any similar schemes which this book has helped to stimulate. Anyone interested in maintaining a dialogue on parental involvement in children's reading is asked to contact the authors, care of the Education Department, West Glamorgan County Council, County Hall, Swansea, SA1 3SN.

Bibliography

ADAMSON, LESLEY (1970) *I Can Write a Story*, Books 1, 2, 3. Leeds and Exeter: Arnold-Wheaton.

ANDREW, P. and PROVIS, W. M. (1983) 'One school's experience in setting up a scheme to involve parents in listening to their children read.' *Links*, Autumn 1983: 26–9.

ARNOLD, H. (1983) *Listening to Children Reading*. London: Hodder and Stoughton.

ATKIN, J. and BASTIANI, J. (1985) *A Survey of Initial Training*. Nottingham: University of Nottingham.

BRANSTON, P. and PROVIS, W. M. (1984a) *Caper: A Resource Pack for West Glamorgan Schools*. Swansea: West Glamorgan County Council.

BRANSTON, P. and PROVIS, W. M. (1984b) *Caper Workshop Pack*. Swansea: West Glamorgan County Council.

BRANSTON, P. and PROVIS, W. M. (1984c) *Caper Clinic Pack*. Swansea: West Glamorgan County Council.

BUSHELL, R. *et al.* (1982) 'Parents as remedial teachers.' *Association of Educational Psychologists Journal*, 5, 9: 7–13.

CHAZAN, M. *et al.* (1976) *Studies of Infant School Deprivation and School Progress*. Oxford: Basil Blackwell.

CLAY, M. M. (1979) *Reading: The patterning of complex behaviour*. London: Heinemann.

CYSTER, R., CLIFT, P. S. and BATTLE, S. (1980) *Parental Involvement in Primary Schools*. Windsor: NFER-Nelson.

DAVIE, R. *et al.* (1972) *From Birth to Seven*. London: Longman.

DEPARTMENT OF EDUCATION AND SCIENCE (1967) *Children and their Primary Schools* (2 vols) (The Plowden Report). London: Her Majesty's Stationery Office (HMSO).

DEPARTMENT OF EDUCATION and SCIENCE (1975) *A Language for Life* (The Bullock Report). London: HMSO.

DEPARTMENT OF EDUCATION AND SCIENCE (1977) *A New Partnership for Our Schools* (The Taylor Report). London: HMSO.

DEPARTMENT OF EDUCATION AND SCIENCE (1984) *Parental Influences* (Green Paper). Cmnd 9494. London: HMSO.

DOUGLAS, J. W. B. (1964) *The Home and the School*. London: MacGibbon and Kee.

EDWARDS, L. and BRANSTON, P. (1979) *Reading, how parents can help*. Swansea: West Glamorgan County Council.

FRIEND, P. (1983) 'Reading and the parent, after the Haringey Reading Project.' *Reading*, 17: 7–12.

GRIFFITHS, A. and HAMILTON, D. (1984) *Parent, Teacher, Child*. London: Methuen.

HANNON, P. W. and CUCKLE, P. (1984) 'Involving parents in the teaching of reading: a study of current school practice.' *Education Research*, 26, 1: 7–13.

HEWISON, J. (1979) 'Home Environment and Reading Attainment. A study of children in a working-class community.' Unpublished Ph.D. thesis, University of London.

HUNT, ALBERT (1972) 'The tyranny of subjects', in Rubinstein, D. and Steinman, C. (eds) *Education of Democracy*. Harmondsworth: Penguin Books.

ILEA Committee on Primary Education (1985) *Improving Primary Schools* (The Thomas Report). London: Inner London Education Authority.

JACKSON, A. and HANNON, P. W. (1980) *The Belfield Reading Project*. Rochdale: Belfield Community Council.

MITTLER, P. and MITTLER, H. (1982) *Partnership with Parents*. Stratford-upon-Avon: National Council for Special Education.

MORGAN, R. and LYON, E. (1979) 'Paired reading: a preliminary report on a technique for parental tuition of reading retarded children.' *Journal of Child Psychology and Psychiatry*, 20: 151–60.

PAYTON, SHIRLEY (1984) *Developing Awareness of Print: A young child's first steps towards literacy. Educational Review* Occasional Publications No. 2. Birmingham: University of Birmingham.

PROVIS, W. M. (1983) *Caper — An Interim Report*. Swansea: West Glamorgan County Council.

PROVIS, W. M. (1984) 'A parental involvement project in one Primary School.' Unpublished M.Ed. thesis, University of Cardiff.

PROVIS, W. M. and ANDREW, P. (1984) 'A parental involvement project.' *Links,* Summer 1984: 24–5.

Schools Council (1968) *Enquiry 1*. London: HMSO.

SOUTHGATE, V. *et al.* (1981) *Extending Beginning Reading*. London: Heinemann.

TIZARD, B. *et al.* (1981) *Involving Parents in Infant and Nursery Schools*. London: Grant McIntyre.

TIZARD, J. *et al.* (1981) 'Collaboration between teachers and parents in assisting children's reading.' *British Journal of Educational Psychology*, 52: 1–15.

WADE, BARRIE (1984) *Story at Home and School. Educational Review* Occasional Publications No. 10. Birmingham: University of Birmingham.

WIDLAKE, P. and MACLEOD, F. (1984) *Raising Standards: Parental Involvement Programmes and the Language Performance of Children*. Coventry: Community Education Development Centre.

YOUNG, M. and MCGEENEY, P. (1968) *Learning begins at Home*. London: Routledge and Kegan Paul.

YOUNG, P. and TYRE, C. (1983) *Dyslexia or Illiteracy?* Milton Keynes: Open University Press.

Appendices

Daily Comment Booklet (pages 103–6)

This is an absolutely essential element of the scheme. Either use this one or produce a modified version. The Caper Comment Booklet assumes that parents will read with their children each evening. Parents are quite willing to make this level of commitment.

Remember to 'personalise' the booklet by printing the name of your class or school on the cover. Do try to make your booklet attractive and professional in appearance. A loose sheet of paper will not give the scheme the best kind of image in children's and parents' eyes.

Instructions for assembling the Daily Comment Booklet

Reproduce the four pages which comprise the Comment Booklet, fold along the dotted lines and stick together in pairs, back to back. Insert the pages of ruled lines within the cover pages and staple the booklet together.

Caper Flipsheet (pages 107–12)

This is the handout given to parents at the initial meeting. It should be personalised with the name of your class or school. It should be modified for the parents of younger nursery or reception class pupils.

The Flipsheet is a worthwhile investment and you are strongly advised to produce one along the lines indicated. The Caper Flipsheet helps to remind parents what was said in the meeting and will be used by parents to explain to other potential helpers at home, unable to attend, what went on.

Instructions for assembling the Caper Flipsheet

Reproduce the six pages which comprise the Caper Flipsheet, fold along the dotted lines and stick together in pairs, back to back. Assemble the booklet by following the numbering of the pages. (Note that Humpty Dumpty forms the centre of the booklet.)

Daily Comment Booklet

The

FOLD

NAME

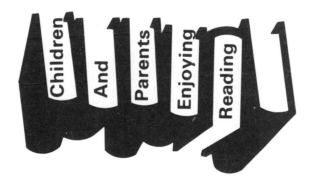

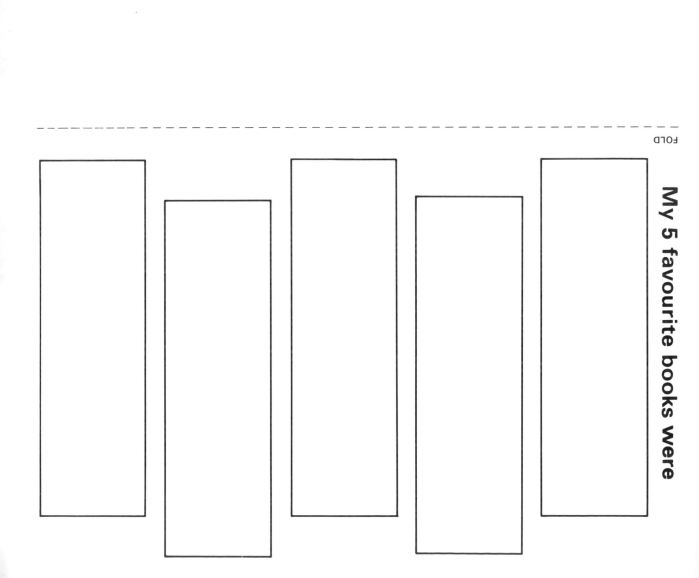

FOLD

My 5 favourite books were

Week	Your Comments	Teacher
1 M		
T		
W		
Th		
F		
Wd		
2 M		
T		
W		
Th		
F		
Wd		
3 M		
T		
W		
Th		
F		
Wd		

Teacher's Comments

FOLD

- -

Week	Your Comments	Teacher
10 M		
T		
W		
Th		
F		
Wd		
11 M		
T		
W		
Th		
F		
Wd		
12 M		
T		
W		
Th		
F		
Wd		

Teacher's Comments

Week	Your Comments	Teacher
4 M		
T		
W		
Th		
F		
Wd		
5 M		
T		
W		
Th		
F		
Wd		
6 M		
T		
W		
Th		
F		
Wd		

Teacher's Comments

FOLD

Week	Your Comments	Teacher
7 M		
T		
W		
Th		
F		
Wd		
8 M		
T		
W		
Th		
F		
Wd		
9 M		
T		
W		
Th		
F		
Wd		

Teacher's Comments

Scoring Key

If you answered YES to the questions, score the following:—

1. one   *2.* one   *3.* one   *4.* One   *5.* three
6a. one   *6b.* nil   *6c.* nil   *6d* two   *7.* one
8. nil   *9.* one   *10.* one   *11.* four
12. three

How did you make out?

Score 16–20   Excellent. You should have no difficulty in helping your child.

10–16   Very good.

4–10   Only average. Room for improvement here!

0– 4   Not too good. Follow the advice in the book and take the test again in 2 or 3 months.

12

FOLD

Helping your child to enjoy
reading

Parents often ask themselves, "How can I help my child read?"

Many are afraid to help in case they interfere with the school's reading approach.

Yet 60% of parents help their children learn to read.

Test yourself

Tick your answers YES or No.

1. I have talked to my child about the book we are reading.	YES / NO
2. I have read the story book myself.	YES / NO
3. My child can tell me what comes next in the story.	YES / NO
4. My child can tell the story in his own words.	YES / NO
5. We read together every night.	YES / NO
6. When my child comes to an unfamiliar word do I—	
a) give it straight away?	YES / NO
b) sound it out?	YES / NO
c) make him sound it out?	YES / NO
d) help him to guess sensibly?	YES / NO
7. My child belongs to and visits the local library.	YES / NO
8. Helping with reading is left to Mum.	YES / NO
9. Before buying a book for my child I read it myself where possible.	YES / NO
10. I like books myself.	YES / NO
11. I can name four children's authors.	YES / NO
12. I am confident my child will be a successful reader.	YES/NO

Other sources of books

LIBRARY

CHILDRENS SECTION

Books can be borrowed through our local library. Ask the Librarian's advice. It is helpful if you know the author or title of the books your child likes.

BOOKSELLERS →

W. H. SMITHS

← *NEWSAGENTS*

CASSETTE

Bookshops

Remember when you buy books to buy those your children like and not the books *you* think they *ought* to read. There is no point in forcing them to read books they do not enjoy or understand.

FOLD

Reading is

fun

exciting

LOOK AND LEARN

CROSS NOW

WAIT

NO ENTRY

STOP

essential

TALKING AND READING

You taught him to talk. You listened to him in turn.

He listened to you.

Then you shared conversations.

We can apply this to reading.

First, read to your child.

FOLD

- -

Your children will always have a book from school at home.

They will have a termly booklet for you to comment in each day. Use the booklet to record their reading and any problems you discover.

Week 1		Your Comments	Teacher's Initials
M	He read well – the story flowed.		
T	Keeps reading 'saw' for 'was'.		
W	We are both excited by this adventure.		
T	Both of us too tired after the supermarket.		

**If s/he gets stuck
on a word ......**

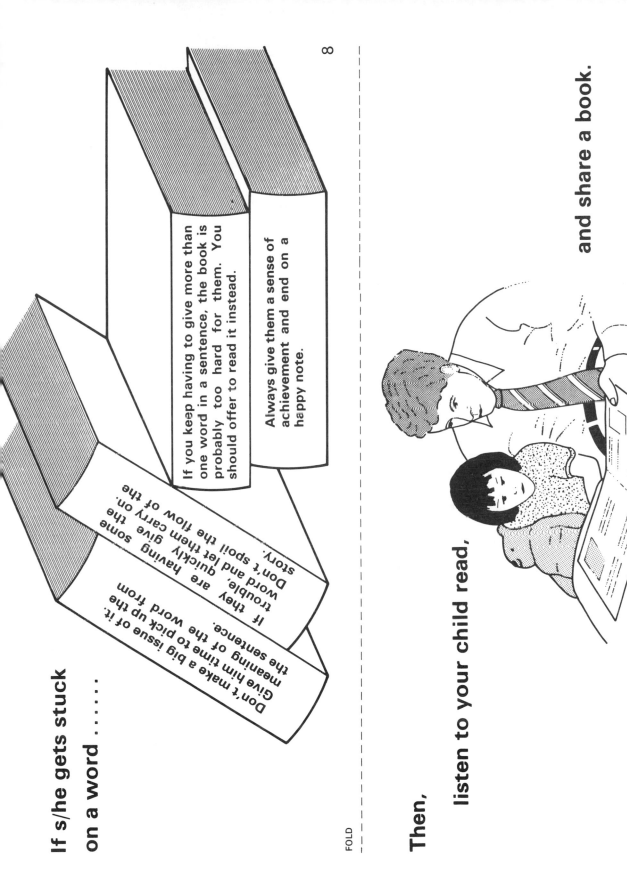

Don't make a big issue of it.
Give him time to pick up the
meaning of the word from
the sentence.

If they are having some
trouble, quickly give the
word and let them carry on.
Don't spoil the flow of the
story.

If you keep having to give more than
one word in a sentence, the book is
probably too hard for them. You
should offer to read it instead.

Always give them a sense of
achievement and end on a
happy note.

FOLD

Then,

listen to your child read,

and share a book.

READING   TOGETHER

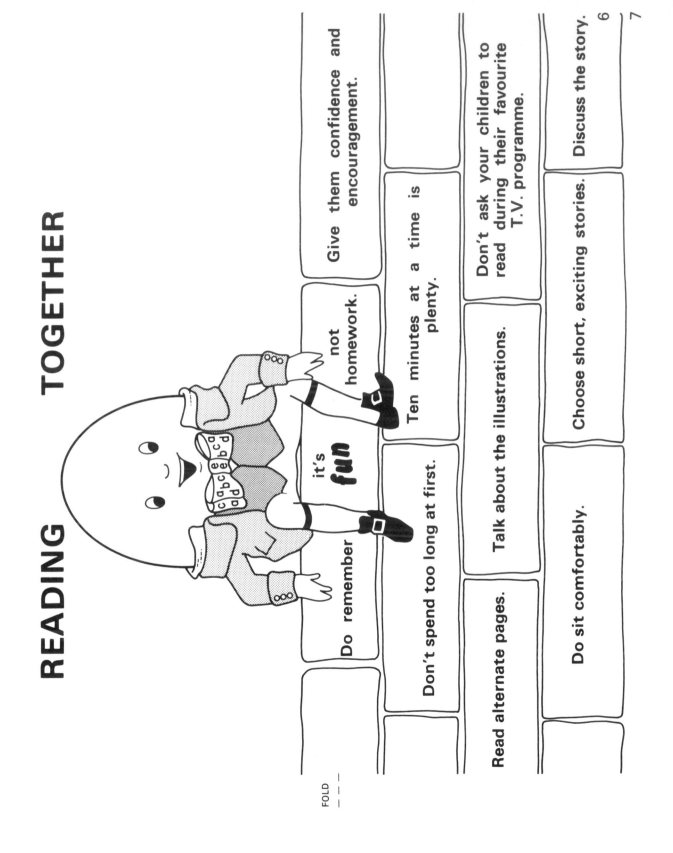

Do remember it's **fun** not homework.

Don't spend too long at first.

Ten minutes at a time is plenty.

Read alternate pages.

Talk about the illustrations.

Give them confidence and encouragement.

Do sit comfortably.

Choose short, exciting stories.

Don't ask your children to read during their favourite T.V. programme.

Discuss the story.

FOLD
‒ ‒ ‒

6

7

Parent Questionnaires 1 and 2

These are the questionnaires used in the Caper scheme so far. The first is used after half term of term one; the second early in term two. They provide a guide to the level of parental support given to the scheme; they also serve as a reminder to parents that the scheme is still very much under way. Give them a try, modified for your own use. The response to the questionnaires is both encouraging and instructive.

Examples are printed on pages 114–16, and may be photocopied freely.

Children's Attitude Scale

Scale One (girl and boy), Scale Two, and Scale Three (girl and boy) are on pages 117–21.

These are easy to construct and test out. The results can be very helpful, both in terms of what they reveal about an individual child, and about how attitudes may be changing over time. Scale One has been used successfully with six- to seven-year-olds but would need to be modified for use with children younger than that. Scale Two can also be used with six- to eight-year-olds. Scale Three is more suited to children who are eight or older.

Mark all the scales by awarding one point for each positive comment. Make a note of each child's total score and compare this with the score the child obtains when re-assessed.

Parent Questionnaire 1

Child's Name _____ Class _____

1 Did you attend one of the reading meetings held by   ?
Yes/No

2 Have you received a copy of the Caper Reading Booklet?   Yes/No

3 Does your son/daughter have a school reading book at home?
constantly _____ occasionally _____ rarely _____ never_____

4 Do you hear him/her read from this book? _____

5 If so, how often?
Daily _____ Every other day _____ Twice a week _____ Less often _____

6 When you hear him/her read, how long does the session last?
5 mins. _____ 10 mins. _____ 15 mins. _____ 20 mins. _____ longer _____

7 Does anyone else hear him/her read?
Mother _____ Father _____ Grandparent _____ Others (please specify) _____

8 What is his/her attitude to these sessions?
Eager to read _____ Unwilling _____ Reluctant to read _____ Refuses _____
Willing to read _____

9 How often does he/she change his/her reading books?
Weekly _____ Fortnightly _____ Monthly _____ Each Half Term _____

10 Do you complete the daily Comment Booklet?   Yes/No

11 Are the books always easy for him/her to read? _____ If not – what do you do?
Read it myself _____ Read it first _____ Let him struggle _____ Return it _____

12 Other than school, does your child have books from other sources?   Yes/No

If yes, where from? _____

_____

13 Have you made contact with teachers in the school regarding your child's reading since the scheme began?   Yes/No

14 What, if any, have been the benefits of this Scheme?

_____

_____

_____

Signed _____ Mother/Father/Guardian

Parent Questionnaire 2

Dear Parent,

In order to help us follow the reading project's progress, could you please fill in the questionnaire below and send it back to school as soon as possible.

Many thanks in anticipation of your co-operation.

---

1 How often does your child have a book home from school?

rarely _____ never _____ constantly _____ occasionally _____

2 How often do you listen to your child read?

Twice a week _____ Daily _____ Every other day _____ Less often _____

3 How long do you listen for?
20 mins. _____ 5 mins. _____ 15 mins. _____ 25 mins. _____ 10 mins. _____

4 Who else listens to your child read?

Mother _____ Father _____ Grandparent _____ Brother, Sister _____

Others (please specify) _____

5 How would you describe your child's attitude to reading aloud to you?

Hesitant _____ Willing _____ Unwilling _____ Eager to read _____ Refuses _____

6 How often do you make a comment in his/her Comment Booklet?

Twice a week _____ Daily _____ Every other day _____ Less often _____

Signed _____ Parent of _____

Girls' Attitude Scale 1

Name: _____ School: _____

Class: _____

Helen is a little girl. She comes to school every day, except weekends and holidays, of course!

Tick the Right Face

1 How does Helen feel when her Mum says "Read this story out loud to me"?

2 How does Helen feel about reading at home?

3 How does Helen feel about reading to her teacher at school?

4 How does Helen feel when her Mum or her teacher reads a story out loud to her?

5 How does Helen feel when she reads to herself (for instance, in bed)?

118

Boys' Attitude Scale 1

Name: _____ School: _____

Class: _____

Peter is a little boy. He comes to school every day, except weekends and holidays, of course!

Tick the Right Face

1 How does Peter feel when his Mum says "Read this story out loud to me"?

2 How does Peter feel about reading at home?

3 How does Peter feel about reading to his teacher at school?

4 How does Peter feel when his Mum or his teacher reads a story out loud to him?

5 How does Peter feel when he reads to himself (for instance, in bed)?

Scale 2

Put a circle around YES or NO

1	Do you like reading books out loud to your mother?	YES	NO
2	Do you like reading at home?	YES	NO
3	Do you like reading at school?	YES	NO
4	When your Mum asks you to read, do you pretend not to hear?	YES	NO
5	When your Mum or your teacher read a story out loud, is that the only time you like books?	YES	NO
6	When your Mum asks you to read, do you sometimes get cross?	YES	NO
7	Are you always reading books?	YES	NO
8	Have you read so many books that you can't remember them all?	YES	NO
9	Do you always tell Mum and Dad about the story you're reading?	YES	NO
10	Do you like reading to yourself, especially in bed, best of all?	YES	NO

The best sort of books are_____

The worst sort of books are_____

Girls' Attitude Scale 3

Name: _____   School: _____

Class: _____

Helen did not like reading books out loud to her Mother (like me/not like me).

She did not like reading at home (like me/not like me), and she did not enjoy reading at school (like me/not like me).

If her Mum asked her to read to her she would pretend not to hear (like me/not like me), or sometimes she would even get cross (like me/not like me).

The only time she liked books was when her Mum or her teacher read a story out loud (like me/not like me).

Her sister Mandy was always reading books (like me/not like me). Mandy had read so many books that she could not remember them all (like me/not like me).

Mandy always told her Mum and Dad about the story she was reading (like me/not like me). She would ask them to listen to her read.

Best of all Mandy liked to read to herself, especially in bed (like me/not like me).

_____

The best sort of books are _____
_____
_____

The worst sort of books are _____
_____
_____

Boys' Attitude Scale 3

Name: _____   School: _____

Class: _____

Peter did not like reading books out loud to his Mother (like me/not like me)

He did not like reading at home (like me/not like me), and he did not enjoy reading at school (like me/not like me).

If his Mum asked him to read to her he would pretend not to hear (like me/not like me), or sometimes he would even get cross (like me/not like me).

The only time he liked books was when his Mum or his teacher read a story out loud (like me/not like me).

His brother David was always reading books (like me/not like me). David had read so many books that he could not remember them all (like me/not like me),

David always told his Mum and Dad about the story he was reading (like me/not like me). He would ask them to listen to him read.

Best of all David liked to read to himself, especially in bed (like me/not like me).

_____

The best sort of books are_____

_____

_____

The worst sort of books are _____

_____

_____